HOW TO GET
Married in
Green

Have an eco-friendly wedding without compromising on style

SUZAN ST MAUR

howtobooks

The paper used for this book is FSC certified and totally chlorine free. FSC (The Forest Stewardship Council) is an international network to promote responsible management of the world's forests.

Published by How To Books Ltd,
Spring Hill House, Spring Hill Road,
Begbroke, Oxford OX5 1RX, United Kingdom
Tel: (01865) 375794. Fax: (01865) 379162
info@howtobooks.co.uk
www.howtobooks.co.uk

How To Books greatly reduce the carbon footprint of their books by sourcing their typesetting and printing in the UK.

British Library Cataloguing in Publication Data
A catalogue record for this book is available from the British Library

ISBN 978 1 84528 270 7

Cover design by Baseline Arts Ltd, Oxford
Produced for How To Books by Deer Park Productions, Tavistock
Typeset by Pantek Arts Ltd, Maidstone, Kent
Printed and bound by Cromwell Press, Trowbridge, Wiltshire

Note: the material contained in this book is set out in good faith for general guidance and no liability can be accepted for loss or expense incurred as a result of relying in particular circumstances on statements made in the book. Laws and regulations are complex and liable to change, and readers should check the current position with the relevant authorities before making personal arrangements.

Contents

Contents

Dedication

To all those people who warned us of the dangers to our planet many years ago — we should have listened to you then.

The author

Canadian-born Suzan St Maur is a researcher, writer and author specialising in business, consumer and humour topics. She has extensive experience of writing across all media in both corporate and entertainment fields, and is also well known as a business and humorous columnist on hundreds of websites internationally. As well as writing her own material she edits other people's books, scripts and text, and advises on book preparation and publication.

She has written 16 published books of her own, including the popular *Wedding Speeches For Women* and *The A to Z of Wedding Worries – and how to put them right*, also by How To Books.

Suzan lives in Bedfordshire, UK, with her teenage son and various pets.

You can read more about Suzan and her work on her website – http://www.suzanstmaur.com

Other books by Suzan St Maur

- The Jewellery Book (*with Norbert Streep*) (Magnum)
- The Home Safety Book (Jill Norman Books)
- The A to Z of Video and AV Jargon (Routledge)
- Writing Words That Sell (*with John Butman*) (Management Books 2000)
- Writing Your Own Scripts and Speeches (McGraw Hill)
- The Horse Lover's Joke Book (Kenilworth Press)

- **Powerwriting** (Prentice Hall Business)
- **Canine Capers** (Kenilworth Press)
- **The Food Lover's Joke Book** (ItsCooking.com)
- **Get Yourself Published** (LeanMarketing Press)
- **The MAMBA Way To Make Your Words Sell** (LeanMarketing Press)
- **The Easy Way To Be Brilliant At Business Writing** (LeanMarketing Press)
- **Wedding Speeches For Women** (How To Books)
- **The Country-Lover's Joke Book** (Merlin Unwin Books)
- **The A to Z of Wedding Worries** (How To Books)

Preface

Hello and welcome to *How To Get Married In Green*.

Before we go any further I want to make myself clear. I am not an environmentalist or, in fact, any kind of expert in saving the planet. But I am an expert in writing about weddings – planning them and preparing speeches for them. And I do care about our planet and the damage we have done to it.

There's an awful lot of waste and extravagance involved in the whole wedding industry.

So my role has been – as someone just like you – to investigate the realities of making your wedding as eco-friendly as possible without losing the style and pizazz you want and rightly deserve, and come up with some ideas on how you can achieve that.

One thing that has struck me more than anything in researching/writing this book has been the plethora of topics concerned within the whole umbrella of "green". Here we're dealing with various, and not necessarily complementary, issues like those connected with:

1. ecological problems

2. our environment

3. sustainable/ethical, fairtrade

4. organic food/drink produce

5. local produce, eco-consumerism

6. energy-reducing initiatives

7. re-use of materials

8. recycling of materials into new products

9. preservation of our wildlife, flora and fauna

10. avoidance — should it be proven undesirable — of GM foods and other produce

11. eco-tourism.

... And that's just for starters.

Often you'll be required to make a choice between one of these elements and another — fairtrade but imported, locally-grown but not organic, organic but expensive, eco-tourism but thousands of miles away, and so-on. When making these decisions, don't forget to factor in cost. Green often means more expensive and you don't want to blow your wedding budget out of proportion — especially if, with a little lateral thinking, you can find an almost-as-green alternative that costs a lot less.

As green issues become increasingly prominent in our day-to-day lives, needless to say there are more and more companies and organisations forming to address those issues on a commercial basis. Along with all the right-minded companies and organisations springing up all over the place there are the odd few wrong-minded ones who seek to take advantage of our keen interest in all things green and exploit that for all they can. Be very careful of this, and use your common sense.

As with most things in life you have to balance everything out and do what you feel is right for the planet, without compromising on what is right for you. And although you may feel you should design your wedding around being as green as possible, don't forget that this is the most important day of your life. The planet will forgive you if you fail to observe every last green restriction. Honest.

Throughout the book I have made suggestions of keywords you should use when searching for information on the internet. If there is more than one word, you will see that I have put inverted commas (quotation marks) on either end of the phrase. This is *not* for decorative or grammatical purposes! Key the inverted commas into the search box as I show them; including them will make your search results more accurate.

Here's wishing you all the best for a wonderful wedding that's both green *and* gorgeous!

Suze
http://www.SuzanStMaur.com

1 Jewellery

As more often than not, getting engaged is the first step in the wedding planning process, I thought it would make sense to start by looking at the green issues surrounding precious jewellery, i.e. for those all important engagement and wedding rings.

A number of awful things have happened and are still happening as a result of precious jewellery components being extracted from the planet.

And having researched the topic at some length for the purposes of this book I now look down at my little diamond or two and think, "I wonder what trouble was caused by you being dug up?"

One perhaps dubious sign that an issue is worthy of serious attention arises when Hollywood makes a movie about it, and the diamond mining industry got its turn with the release of "Blood Diamond" starring Leonardo DiCaprio in 2006. The movie, in which an impecunious African farming type finds himself in an uncomfortable clinch between the syndicate controlling his local diamond industry and a US diamond smuggler, took over US $57 million in the first instance at the US box office. So blood diamonds are finally on the map.

(As it happens, all things "eco" are important to Leonardo DiCaprio; he is very active in conservation and environmental fields. You can learn more on his website: http://www.leonardodicaprio.org.)

However, it is not just diamonds and their mining which can wreak havoc with the environment and innocent people's lives; gold, silver and platinum mining have their horror stories, as does mining for other precious gemstones. Before we look at what we can do to minimise our own jewellery impact on people and the planet, let's take a slightly deeper look at the actual problems.

Diamonds

Little did Marilyn Monroe know when she sang about "diamonds are a girl's best friend", that they could also be her worst. Being small, highly portable and easy to conceal as well as internationally precious, **"blood" or "conflict" diamonds** have become an international currency for a wide variety of rebel-inspired human atrocities. They have been traded for the funding of civil conflict and wars resulting in, amongst other things, the displacement and death of several million people throughout Africa, plus the funding of numerous terrorist organisations and of course, money-laundering. Organised crime and tax evasion are two further activities often underpinned by diamonds. At the peak of this activity somewhere between 4% and 15% – depending on whose statistics you look at – of total world diamond trade was down to blood diamonds. No wonder the film-makers took such an interest.

However, the world's watchdogs took an interest somewhat earlier than the film-makers and after several years of international pressure, the Kimberley Process Certification Scheme was created by various govern-ments in 2003 to attempt to control the problem. Around 70 countries are now members. With all the goodwill in the world, though, the Kimberley Process can only make life more difficult for the rebels who have been using diamonds as a currency for their monstrosities. Blood diamonds are still around, and are likely to continue to be around for some time to come.

The horrors don't stop there, either. The act of **diamond mining** in itself can cause environmental disaster. A lot depends on the methods used for mining and in fairness, the larger organisations now use technology and pollution control to minimise the impact. However, in the smaller operations, often in the poorer African countries, diamond mining still causes a range of environmental problems including inadequate waste disposal, dust pollution, fuel oil and other chemical pollution due to explosives used, pollution from hydrocarbon based fuels and lubricants, soil erosion, destruction of vegetation, flooding, ground water pollution and in some cases pollution of drinking water as well, leading to increased cases of cholera, dysentery and malaria-carrying mosquitoes.

And as if that weren't enough, the production end of the diamond industry is not all sweetness and light, either. A significant percentage of the world's diamond output receives its initial cutting and polishing in countries like India, where you frequently see children doing the work for very little money.

Still want that brand new diamond? If you have your heart set on the "real thing", at least ensure that the diamond was mined in Canada. Unlike many other countries, Canada has strict environmental laws relating to their diamond mines — and those are rigorously enforced. From the human point of view, too, the diamond mines are beneficial. Mostly the diamond deposits are found in the north of Canada which does not have the friendliest climate in the world and consequently local people find it hard to scratch a living. Mining companies in these regions are legally obliged to employ nearly 70% of their staff from local communities, of whom at least half must be Aboriginals. Pay and working conditions are good. But despite careful regulation — and restitution - they're still digging up the landscape.

Other precious gemstones

Many of us prefer a coloured stone for our engagement rings, rather than the traditional diamond. In the bad old days when I wrote my first ever book (co-authored with gemmologist Norbert Streep) — "The Jewellery Book" — we knew diamonds, emeralds, rubies and sapphires as "precious stones" with the rest as "semi-precious". Nowadays I believe they're all called gemstones, which undoubtedly is more democratic. However, for an engagement ring many of us would probably choose an emerald, ruby or sapphire as an alternative to a diamond, rather than previously-entitled semi-precious stones like citrine, topaz, aquamarine, peridot, opal, etc.

Jewellery

The horrors continue, however.

Needless to say, it's not merely diamonds that act as a very convenient and portable currency for illegal, and often murderous, activities. In south-east Asia there is a burgeoning use of **various different gemstones** connected with just about every organised criminal activity you can think of. Not all of these are necessarily bad for our environment, but many cause death, sickness and deprivation to thousands of innocent people.

Ruby and sapphire mining is widely practised in Australia and there environmental watchdogs have somewhat more bite than they do in "developing" countries. This activity can chew up land for miles and risk polluting rivers and water supplies, especially as the mining process can involve drilling down into river beds. At Barrington Tops, a World Heritage wilderness park in New South Wales, Australia, there has been a struggle going on for some time in the whole area to constrain mining for rubies, sapphires and zircons, most of which are found in river beds. The waterways in this area supply clean water for about one million people, and environmentalists are understandably sceptical that the water can stay clean when mining organisations are drilling into the river beds all over the place, and mining around 250 tonnes each day.

In other areas of Australia sapphire mining is now being done with much more care for the environment. One typical new-style operation, described as "shallow open cut mining", involves making a small cut in the land, a metre or two wide. Topsoil is carefully removed and put to one side. The digger moves along the line and as it finishes a section, the gap is carefully filled in, topsoil replaced, and vegetation is replanted. At any one time the hole in the ground created by the mining exercise never gets any bigger than two or three metres across.

All that's very encouraging, but Australia in some ways is but a small voice in the wilderness. In other countries, particularly those with poorer economies and less active social consciences, gemstone mining not only funds crime and wars but also destroys everything in its path. In South America for example, "strip mining" for emeralds digs out acres and acres of vegetation and topsoil. And unlike in well-supervised Australia, very little gets put back. What that leads to is soil erosion, degradation of rivers, loss of habitat for wildlife, deforestation and general pollution.

Precious metals

According to some statistics, to make one simple gold ring creates up to 20 tons of mine waste; each ounce of finished gold is responsible for about 30 tons. Put simply, when it comes to bad news, gold mining takes the first prize. It's known to be one of the worst mining industries of all in terms of destruction and the disasters it causes, greedily kicking indigenous people out of the their communities, damaging the environment and polluting the local water supply to the point of poisoning it.

Although some **gold mining** is done on the basis of underground shafts this method is expensive. As a result the majority of gold mining is of the open pit variety, which naturally chops up large swathes of land. This is done using not only machinery but also explosives. Open pit mines create up to 10 times the amount of waste than that of the underground shaft method.

One of the most charming constituents of much gold mining is the use of cyanide. This is sprayed on to the crushed ore which is piled up in "heaps". The cyanide bonds with any gold in the ore and the two together run through the heap, being collected when they reach the bottom. This process is called "heap leaching". Once the gold and cyanide are separated the cyanide is kept in artificial ponds and eventually re-used. (Nice to know they at least recycle that.)

Given the scale of this leaching process and the fact that it takes a matter of months to get through each cycle, it's inevitable that some of this poison finds its way into the local environment and ecosystems. And until very recently, when gold mines were located near a sea coast the most popular and widely used dumping grounds for this tasty waste was in the ocean. Many countries now are tightening up regulations for this but as we know, some countries are better at caring for the planet than others.

Platinum, another popular choice for the mounting of engagement rings and also for making wedding rings, has a similarly controversial environmental profile. Recently, the demand for this metal has increased dramatically; not for use in jewellery, but for use in car components to supply the growing demand for cars in countries like India and China.

Most of the world's platinum comes from South Africa and although much has been done there to reduce the way mining affects the local environment and communities, there is still considerable concern.

One potential problem area is groundwater. Platinum mining in this part of Africa involves pumping out millions of gallons of water underground every year. A lot of that is reused for mining, but all the same there are fears of eventual leaching into the ground of all sorts of undesirable elements, including the possibility of heavy metal seepage. Not good for the local water supply.

Some people also fear that acid mine drainage via residue and waste dumping could create bad pollution, and acid rain is a possibility due to various emissions. Already it is being said that the rate of respiratory infections amongst the indigenous population has increased.

So, that's the bad news

As I've said there are moves afoot in many countries where gemstone and precious metal mining takes place, to reduce both human and geographical intrusion and its consequent effects. But realistically, within the shelf life of this book it's unlikely that such mining will be brought under total control, especially in smaller, developing countries where even the long arm of the law does not quite reach as far as it could.

What can we do? It depends how green you want to be.

Recycled precious metals

It's ironic to think that, sitting in bank vaults and under mattresses all over the world, lie thousands and thousands of tons of hoarded gold in the form of jewellery and also as ingots, or gold bars. Some say there is enough in these hidey-holes to keep the world's gold demand satisfied for anything up to 50 years without mining another ounce.

A large percentage of gold is used to make jewellery, but also we must remember that gold has been pegged to the world's economy for centuries. So it's an economic, as well as political hot potato.

Despite the hoarding, there is now quite a large market for **recycled gold**, made up mostly of old jewellery that has been melted down and refinished. The best way to ensure that your wedding and engagement rings are properly made from recycled precious metal is to supply a professional jeweller with some old jewellery of yours to be melted down and reused. With commercially produced recycled gold, although it's almost certainly respectable, it still doesn't come with precise knowledge of where it originated.

It may be that there are rings on one or other side of your families which could be remodelled and/or resized. Not only does this act as recycling of the jewellery, but also carries on a lovely tradition. I now wear the wedding ring that was my late mother's, and before that my late grandmother's. It dates back to my grandparents' wedding way back in ...oh, let's not go there, but it was a long time ago!

Secondhand jewellery

Some people are a little superstitious about buying and wearing second-hand jewellery, especially in the case of emotionally important engagement and wedding rings. If this does not worry you, however, not only is this a green thing to do but also it can save you a lot of money.

Most of the money you pay for new jewellery is for the work involved in mining, processing, designing and manufacturing the item. The value of the metal and stones represents a small fraction of the total retail price. If you were to buy a brand new diamond ring and take it to a second-hand dealer ten minutes later, you would be offered merely the scrap value of the metal and stones and very little else.

Obviously, when you buy secondhand jewellery you will be paying somewhat more than its scrap value, because there is the secondhand jeweller's profit to be taken into consideration — that's commerce for you. All the same, this time the costs of mining, processing, designing and manufacturing have already been paid for. So unless the dealer is very greedy, the asking price will be a fraction of what you'd pay for the same item new.

Because of reasons we would prefer not to think about right now, there will always be a supply of **secondhand engagement rings** — and to a lesser extent wedding rings — on the market. To buy and use second-hand jewellery will not compensate for whatever environmental destruction and human suffering might have been caused by its original production. However, by recycling jewellery rather than buying new, we may send a message to precious metal and gemstone miners and dealers that we're still not happy with the way many of them work.

Manmade gemstones

There is a huge array of manmade stones out there in the jewellery world now, made by a variety of different processes. Some are more effective than others; some purport to be chemically identical to the real thing; some purport to be better than the real thing; some imitate the real thing. You'll see them referred to as "simulated", "synthetic", "laboratory grown", "laboratory created", etc.

From a green point of view, the best news about these created gemstones is that acres of countryside have not been ripped up to get hold of them, and with luck no humans or wildlife have been displaced, menaced or otherwise harmed in their acquisition. Also, created gemstones are normally a lot cheaper than their natural equivalents. Unfortunately, some energy is required to make these stones in the laboratories, but in all probability this does not create such a fat carbon footprint as mining does.

Created gemstones consist of chemical, optical and physical properties that are very similar to their natural equivalents, and are made using one of a number of different methods. The "flame fusion" technique, for example, takes powdered ingredients and fuses them together using a high-temperature flame. The hydrothermal technique puts the ingredients in water which is then heated until they dissolve, then cooled again so that crystals form. The "flux-melt" method, though expensive, results in stones that are very hard to tell from the real thing.

Simulated gemstones are those which do not have similar or the same chemical and other properties as the real thing, and in effect can be anything from something really nice, to a bit of glass or plastic.

One of the most commonly seen manmade stone today is **cubic zirconia**, or CZ. This supplanted YAG (Yttrium Aluminium Garnet) and strontium titanate, earlier simulated diamond substances, in the 1970s and is infinitely superior in colour, clarity, light refraction and everything else. Created in the laboratory, CZ is extremely hard — not as hard as diamond, but almost as hard as sapphire and ruby — and has very good brilliance. Initially just marketed as a diamond substitute and a fairly expensive one at that, the cost of CZ has come right down to supermarket fashion jewellery level. However, it's not junk, and has earned its place as a pretty good diamond alternative. Modern CZ is also available in a number of different colours.

In the mid 1990s, however, CZ was knocked off its perch as the number one artificial gemstone by the superior **moissanite**. Originally a natural stone found in a meteor crater in the United States around the turn of the nineteenth/twentieth centuries, by 1995 its formulation was being created in laboratories. Moissanite stones today are not as cheap as CZ, but still cost only about 10% of what you'd pay for the real thing. And many people swear that even an expert can't tell the difference between moissanite and diamond — certainly not with the naked eye, anyway.

If you choose to buy an engagement ring containing manmade gemstones, or a wedding ring in the form of an eternity ring, do your homework carefully. There are many jewellers and dealers around who are less than honest, and you can be taken in very easily. Look up your options on the internet by entering the appropriate keywords into your favourite search engine, and have a look in jewellery and department stores who can't afford to have their reputations tarnished.

Non-metallic rings

A growing trend amongst avidly green enthusiasts is to forego precious metals altogether and instead have personalised **wedding rings made out of wood**. Now this idea, arguably, is not necessarily that green when you consider that trees may have to be sacrificed in the production process. However, I have found a good many wooden ring makers on the internet saying that they used only salvaged wood, and in any case with appropriate replanting even the creation of several million weddings rings is hardly going to raze a rain forest to the ground.

Much as this idea may sound like a bizarre – and potentially short-lived – choice of material, those who make wooden wedding rings usually supply owners with special wax to ensure the items' longevity.

Some of the designs are really quite beautiful, combining two or three bands of different woods together. Often the wood is locally sourced, and the makers will supply you with a full history of the forest, wood or copse from which your rings were derived. Others will make the rings for you from new or salvaged wood from the area in which you live, or in which your wedding is to take place. Nearly all are made by hand to your own design and currently you can expect to pay between £50 and £100 per ring.

Currently there are only a couple of UK-based wooden wedding ring makers listed on Google, but as the trend grows I'm sure there will be more. Already there are a large number of such makers in North America, so it's only a matter of a short time before Britain follows suit.

Jewellery

What you can do

Engagement rings:

- If buying a new diamond, ensure it was mined in Canada or other fairtrade location.

- Avoid coloured gemstones unless you know where and how they were mined.

- Buy a secondhand or antique ring.

- Have a new ring remodelled from one or more old pieces.

- Use a family heirloom ring, remodelled and/or resized.

- Ensure metal is recycled, not new.

- Buy a ring with a manmade gemstone.

Wedding rings:

- Buy new rings made from commercially recycled gold.

- Have new rings made from melted-down gold of your own.

- Have wooden wedding rings made.

2 Hen and Stag Parties

The tradition of the stag night goes back some centuries, and many say that its origins come from an attempt to ward off evil spirits. Some claim that stag parties took place in Sparta in the fifth century BC, when soldiers would drink multiple toasts the night before a buddy's wedding. Another folklore story says that in the old days the groom was responsible for arranging the stag night celebrations. However, if he did not turn up for the wedding – perhaps as a result of a hangover? – it was the best man's duty to marry the bride instead. Girls, be warned.

On to the female equivalents now and interestingly, although we may think that **hen parties** are a twentieth century evolution arising from feminism, sexual/gender equality and all that, it appears that the idea goes right back to the time of King Charles II in the seventeenth century. These occasions were used by the bride and female relatives and friends to take a good look at the "trousseau", or wedding gifts for the bottom drawer ... not unlike the "bridal showers" common in North America today, but which are still a rarity in the UK and Europe at the time of writing. Whether or not they involved copious boozing and stripping butlers one cannot surmise, but I have a sneaky feeling that such things might have been on the agenda even all those years ago.

We must, of course, pay attention to readers outside of the UK and include the names they use for these occasions in case anyone is in doubt concerning what I'm talking about. We call them "hen" and "stag" occasions here in the UK as well as Ireland, New Zealand and Canada, but in the USA, for example, they can be known as "bachelor" and "bachelorette" parties. And in Australia, I'm told they're called "bucks nights/parties", and in South Africa, "bulls' parties". I'm tempted to ponder what the female equivalents might be in the last two cases but my instincts tell me not to go there ...

Getting back to our green issues, one thing you might find very encouraging — I did subsequent to my research, although (a) I'm too old for such things and (b) I'm married already — is that **outdoor sports** and especially "extreme" sports are becoming very popular for hen and stag sessions. The good news is, many of them are particularly eco-friendly.

In our increasingly health conscious times, fewer and fewer engaged couples see the sense in going out on the town and getting ridiculously drunk, although that still has an appeal in some ways. More frequently though, people like to combine outdoor or at least non-alcoholic daytime activities with, perhaps, tasty dinners and a lot of booze in the evenings. You can still enjoy an evening or evenings of garish entertainment with female/male strippers, excruciatingly strong cocktails and embarrassing karaoke, while at least not having polluted the region with fuel fumes or other noxious substances during the day.

For many people, too, the hen or stag night/weekend/week away is not just about getting drunk and disrupting a foreign community with the loud singing of all 144 verses of "Eskimo Nell". These occasions are also about **bonding** – especially for members of the two families being joined by the forthcoming wedding. And don't forget, the guest lists for these occasions are not always restricted to youthful folks of the bride or groom's generations; it may be necessary, and indeed desirable, to choose activities that can be enjoyed by **people of different age groups**.

Green hen and stag parties: the basics

As with nearly everything else nowadays, there is a wealth of information about hen and stag celebrations on the internet. To find solutions in abundance, it's merely a matter of entering the appropriate keywords into your favourite search engine. In this chapter, however, I have flagged up a selection of things you might like to contemplate, all of which **do not involve anything but limited travel or motorised content** within the activities themselves.

Before we get into all that though, what are the key elements you should consider if you want your hen or stag celebration to damage the planet as little as possible?

1. Do you *really* need to go away in an aircraft that spews awful substances into the atmosphere? If you do, at least pick a

location and type of travel that falls within the boundaries of eco-tourism, and make sure you offset it. There's more on that in Chapter 14, so I won't go into it here.

2. Try if you can to find activities and amenities that do not involve you and your fellow partiers in travelling beyond your locality, if possible.

3. And if you must travel within the UK, select a location that's easily reached by public transport. (Look on the bright side; it's likely that you can all start drinking earlier than were you to drive there.)

So how can we be green and still paint the town red?

In all honesty, there's nothing particularly un-green about going to a local bar or club (especially if you walk there) and getting drunk, especially if it's on organic British booze! But hey — there's more to having fun than that; you can keep it green into the bargain and, as I mentioned earlier, you can still go out for some serious drinking afterwards if you want to.

All that I list below is offered by many organisers of hen and stag occasions, so check them out on your favourite search engine by entering "stag and hen parties". Often you'll find that a combination of a few of these activities is offered as a package, too.

Abseiling

Yes, I know this one has been done to death but there is still a thrill (so I'm told — I'm too chicken to try it) in bouncing down those slippery slopes with only a rope or two to keep you from the depths. UK locations: numerous.

Archery

If you've always fancied your hand at being a Robin Hood or William Tell, and your companions are up for an interesting time as well, there are many options for archery days and weekends in the UK. Key "archery packages" into your favourite UK search engine for current offerings. UK locations: numerous.

Assault course/high ropes

Nothing new here but still a fun challenge whether you're a fit, sporty type or not. Various companies in the UK offer days or weekend variants, many tailored for hen and stag celebrations. UK locations: numerous.

Boating

If you're not the extreme sports type but still like to get out in the fresh air and the countryside, there are many options for small-scale cruising on the UK's waterways. Even outside the summer season, hiring a "narrow boat" and spending a lazy few days gently ambling along, say, the Grand Union canal or the Norfolk Broads is a great way for adults of all ages to bond and enjoy good company. Yes, the boats do have engines which burn fuel, but at a relatively modest level — certainly creating far less damage than an aircraft flying to Majorca and back. UK locations: various.

Canyoning

Now here's a new one for those of us living in Britain, largely because we don't call canyons "canyons" — we're more likely to talk about "gorges" or "ravines". However the sport is more about the waterways running along the bottom of such canyons; to be precise, travelling along them. This you do by a variety of means including scrambling, walking, abseiling, climbing, swimming, and sitting or crouching on an inflatable mattress. UK locations: North Wales, Scotland.

Caving

Not for the faint-hearted, or at least wimps like me who suffer from claustrophobia, but a wonderful activity for those who do not fear confined spaces. Some of the sights in these caves are stunningly beautiful and well worth the scramble to get there. UK locations: Yorkshire Dales, Peak District, Wales, South-West, Northern Ireland, Scotland, Isle of Man, Channel Isles, etc.

Climbing (rock)

Ah, now you're talking. Despite being an old f*rt now at one time in my dim and distant past I enjoyed rock climbing, although the winter alternative with the crampons and thermal everything didn't really grab me. Nowadays you can go rock climbing on an artificial face that's not only supervised by expert staff but also offers central heating to keep you from shivering and, usually, at best an ice cream source or at worst (if you're organically minded) a McDonalds outlet next door. Despite the imminent Big Macs, the activity is just as challenging as it always was, however. And many hen and stag occasion suppliers offer climbing weekends and weeks in the UK. UK locations: numerous, indoor and outdoor.

Coasteering

You need to be pretty bold and brave for this one as essentially it involves jumping off cliffs into the sea, albeit in well reconnoitred and safe locations. More information is available from: http://www.british-coasteeringfederation.co.uk. UK locations: various, particularly along the coasts of the South-West, Wales, Scotland, Northern Ireland.

Dancing

This is a very popular activity and various classes have sprung up almost everywhere in the last few years for such dance genres as Salsa, Jive, Flamenco, Line, Latin, Belly, Ballroom and many more. At the time of writing, there are several companies offering dance packages in the UK, plus many more offering dance weeks in foreign locations (but don't forget to consider the aircraft emissions damage). Key "dance holi-days"+UK into your favourite search engine. UK locations: various.

Falconry

This is a fascinating activity, albeit a little blood-thirsty in its origins, but it's about the way nature works in the wild. It is wonderful to watch how the birds relate to their "prey" (in these demonstrations, usually a stuffed toy) and the opportunity to work the birds yourself is a joy. UK locations: numerous.

Fencing

A challenging sport but one — the basics of which — you can learn on a relatively quick basis. Needless to say it's perfectly safe and the only thing likely to receive a dent is your ego. The sport is quite tightly regu-lated in the UK so if you want to arrange a fencing tuition weekend, say, you would probably need to do it in association with one of the many fencing clubs in the UK. Contact: http://www.britishfencing.com, Tel: 020 8742 3032, Email: enquiries@britishfencing.com.

Football and rugby

Assuming you and the rest of your party all support the same football or rugby team, an obvious choice of weekend away is a trip to watch your team play — preferably at home, so you don't need to travel far, but if "away" then by public transport, please. Also, if you're all keen amateur players, you might like to look into the possibility of organising a five-a-side tournament of your own, in your local park. UK locations: too many even to contemplate!

Frisbee disc golf

This is a new twist on the traditional format of golf (see below) ... instead of hitting a ball with a club, you throw a Frisbee disc. Other than that somewhat crucial difference the rest of the game is pretty much similar. At the time of writing, there are about 1,200 courses around the world and just under 20 in the UK. Some companies offer packages for hen and stag celebrations. Key "Frisbee disc golf" into your favourite search engine. Current UK locations: Aylesbury, Beaminster, Bristol, Colchester, Crieff, Edinburgh, Fife, Greenford, Hayling Island, Inverness, Leamington Spa, London, Malvern, Mull, Oxford, Sheffield, St Andrews, Ullapool, Whitfield.

Golf

Oh, not that old chestnut, I hear you groan, but hang on a minute. Golf is still one of the most popular sports in the UK and despite having gained a reputation as an "old man's game" has an awful lot of young supporters, both male and female. Golf courses are environmentally rea-sonable and shouldn't involve you in much travel to get there as there are so many of them in Britain. And they're ideal if your group consists of different ages.

Health spa

Some of these places are more eco-friendly than others, but do offer the advantage of being within a short travelling distance of most UK towns and certainly offer a glorious way for a busy bride (or groom, although men tend to think this is a bit "girlie") and her friends and female relatives to relax and de-stress before the Big Day. Many of these resorts at least offer organic cosmetics and local produce in their restaurants, which helps.

Mountain biking

Something that's popular as a leisure pursuit on a regular basis for many people, it can also provide an amusing weekend or day out even if you're not a regular participant. You don't have to be an expert. There are many mountain biking and other cycling options available for weekends and longer breaks, so key "mountain biking holidays" into your favourite search engine for more information. NB: you don't need mountains to do mountain biking — only slopes, so there should be a location near you that can provide the venue you need without travelling to the mountains. UK locations: numerous.

Mountain boarding

This is a little more adventurous than mountain biking and requires a somewhat stronger constitution — but those who do it can't sing its praises enough. In fact it is similar in nature to snowboarding, but in this case you roll down a hillside on wheels rather than a flat surface on snow, and/or roll along other surfaces and perform tricks if you're an expert. Also known as "all terrain boarding", it is often described as a cross between snow boarding and skate boarding and is much enjoyed by the young and — so I'm told — you can learn the basics in a relatively short time. All you need is good balance and a lot of guts. Key "mountain boarding" into your favourite search engine for more information. UK locations: various.

Murder weekend

Not exactly a new idea but a great favourite, especially in the winter months when the weather isn't all that appealing for outdoor pursuits. Also they are ideal for a group of mixed ages, interests and physical abilities. As you know, these involve actors playing out a "grisly" murder setup and you and your group must be the detectives and solve the crime. All good clean fun, especially with tasty (organic) meals and plenty of (organic) drinks. Some companies offer murder evenings as well as weekends, and some will also organise an event for you at a venue of your choice. So if you want to ensure the event is green, you can select a venue you know to be eco-conscious and serve only organic, locally-sourced produce. UK locations: numerous.

Orienteering

This has been a popular sport for some years and essentially is a kind of treasure hunt, although I'm sure its exponents would jump down my throat and tell me I'm being offensive to reduce it merely to that ... Anyway, participants aim to reach a distant point via the shortest possible route in the shortest possible time using a specific type of map, controlled at checkpoints along the way. If you like the great outdoors this is a good one. Also because you can progress at your own pace it's appropriate for mixed ages and abilities. It's more usually practised in rural locations but the method can work in urban areas, parks, etc. You'll find more information at: http://www.britishorienteering.co.uk. UK locations: numerous.

Paragliding and hang gliding

A number of companies offer paragliding and hang gliding weekends around the UK and this is tremendous fun, almost irrespective of your age or physical capabilities. These activities usually do require you to jump off a hill or similar so you need to have an enterprising outlook on life but I'm assured that it really doesn't take much in the way of bravery. There are many options available to choose from, so key in "paragliding weekends" as your starter on your favourite search engine. UK locations: various.

Parakarting

This sport is closely related to sand yachting, which has been a favoured activity for some time now. It's an interesting activity that is becoming popular for stag celebrations, although maybe not so much for hen equivalents! Look it up on your favourite search engine. UK locations: various, but bear in mind that a shallow, flat beach is required.

Pony trekking

This is an all-time favourite of mine because I love horses, riding, and the countryside. But don't be put off if you've never been on a horse before; most treks include at least two or three people who are out on a horse for the first time and, because the horses or ponies are very quiet and gentle, the newbies enjoy themselves thoroughly (although they may have some stiff muscles the next day!). There is a wide variety of pony trekking days, weekends and longer holidays available, mostly in the UK's prime beauty spots like Brecon Beacons in South Wales, the New Forest, the Highlands of Scotland, etc. However those are normally accessible by public transport so your group should not need to travel by car. For safety's sake, you would do well to select a trekking yard that's approved by the British Horse Society (http://www.bhs.org.uk) or the Association of British Riding Schools (http://www.abrs-info.org).

Pottery making

This is a popular activity for children's parties but adult versions do exist and are equally popular — there's nothing like rolling up your sleeves and digging with your hands into that clay. And this could be an ideal opportunity to make some bespoke favours for the wedding reception. Just make sure you leave time for a good manicure before the wedding day! Several UK companies offer inclusive courses, weekends, days, etc. Key "pottery parties" into your favourite search engine. UK locations: numerous.

Take a class

How about organic UK wine tasting? Or organic beer tasting? Or how to make wedding decorations, jewellery, etc? Or how to do Thai massage? These things are always enjoyable, especially if you're sharing them with your closest friends and relatives. Check in your local paper and news websites for information about what's available in your area. If you make friends with a local supplier of organic beer or wine, they may be willing to organise a tasting session for you and your party, on the assumption that they may sell some produce as a result. Similarly local origami artists, floral arrangers, jewellery makers, Thai massage instructors, etc. may be willing to set up a private day or weekend for your group. UK locations: numerous.

Tennis, badminton, squash, etc

If you and your hen or stag partiers all play one of these games, you could organise a tournament at your local club, or using a private facility. Healthy, little travel, and no noxious fumes from the activity. UK locations: numerous.

Treasure hunt

I know this may sound a bit like an activity for a child's birthday party, but the adult versions can be a lot of fun and are very unlikely to disrupt local wildlife or burn fuel. The hunts take place on foot and can be themed as anything from Sherlock Holmes to Long John Silver to Prince Charming. Various companies offer treasure hunt packages either in scheduled UK towns and cities, or on private grounds to your own specification. UK locations: numerous.

White water rafting

Despite the British Isles appearing to be relatively gentle in geographical terms, in fact there is a surprisingly large number of waterways lively enough to provide good white water rafting. And where none exists, in some places manmade courses have been built. Like many others within the "extreme" sports bracket, the white water rafting option is available widely by companies offering hen and stag celebrations and often, it's in combination with other outdoor, non-mechanical activities. UK locations: many in Scotland and Wales, some elsewhere.

And that's just a few among a much larger green choice

When I was researching for this chapter, I discovered not only all these green options I have described, but also many more too. The list is endless, but it would be inappropriate to go on at longer length here in this book. Suffice it to say that there are many, many choices of fun activities that do not involve polluting anything — without travelling long distances even on public transport, never mind in an aircraft.

Hen and stag nights

What you can do

- If you must go abroad, ensure you balance the trip with appropriate carbon offset (see Chapter 14).

- If going abroad, make the trip according to eco-tourism recommendations (see Chapter 14).

- If going to continental Europe, go overland (with ferry or tunnel crossing) rather than by air.

- Choose a location within the UK as close as possible to home.

- Travel to the location by public transport if possible.

- Choose an activity that does not involve burning fuel or using too much power.

- Choose an activity that does not involve damaging the environment or wildlife habitat.

3 Location

If you have your heart set on a wedding on a beach in the Caribbean surrounded by several dozen of your closer friends and relatives, the occasion is hardly going to be environmentally friendly even if you all wear locally-made sarongs and no shoes. Bottom-line says that trans-porting yourselves and even a few attendants and family/friends will result in an aviation pollution *bleurrrgghh* of many times that which any of us should contemplate.

Combining wedding and honeymoon: does this help?

In a word, yes. It does. A bit. But even if it's just you and your intended jetting off to an exotic location in the tropical or sub-tropical wild blue yonder, you will need to assuage your consciences by ensuring that you offset the air journey there and back. For example, should you and your fiancé decide to fly from London to Jamaica for your wedding, the emis-sions you'd be responsible for amount to well over 4 tonnes of CO_2. At the current rate, it costs over £30 to offset that. Invite your (4) parents plus the best man and one bridesmaid to join you, and you're looking at almost 17 tonnes of CO_2 with an offset cost of nearly £130. And even if, say, four of you fly to Barcelona for your wedding, there will still be over 1 tonne of CO_2 spewed out and your offset cost will be nearly £8.

And before you start thinking that handing over the cost of a good bottle of wine to offset your flight pollution to Barcelona and back is well worthwhile, ponder this. Just how effective is it if you do hand over offset money in compensation? Increasingly, there is talk in the media of carbon offset schemes and companies mushrooming up all over the place, and while all may be keen to take your money to plant a few new trees in Nicaragua, not all are quite as altruistic as you would want them to be. Carbon offset has now become potentially profitable business, and as such is beginning to attract its fair share of snake-oil salesmen. Anyway, enough about this now as I go into more detail about it all in

Chapter 14, but the message here is, if you want even to be greenish, choose a wedding location – *and* a honeymoon location – somewhat nearer home.

Home, sweet home

Although at first glance your own home – or the (large) home of a close relative – might seem to be a green choice, it probably **isn't the greenest choice** you could make. Unless the home in question is pretty unusual, it won't have the facilities and equipment on hand to cope with the cooking, food, drinks, seating, etc. and all the necessary items will have to be brought in, perhaps from some distance away. That adds to the pollution load. It's true that putting a marquee up in a garden should not cause any lasting damage to the lawn and surrounding areas, but it's surprising just how much damage a few dozen tipsy wedding guests can cause to flower beds and vegetable gardens. Plus, should your wedding take place at any time other than mid-summer (and even then we're being optimistic for the UK) the marquee may need to be heated, which is incredibly wasteful and uses a great deal of power or fuel.

Unless your wedding is to be very small, there are other reasons why having it at home is probably not a good idea, not least of which is the stress and chaos that such an activity causes. This is hardly welcome when the run-up to the wedding in itself can be stressful enough without the added angst of caterers, florists, table servers, bartenders and various others leaping around like headless chickens. Also, people often find that there is little or no cost saving by having a wedding at home; bringing in all the necessary supplies and suppliers can end up costing more than if you take your wedding to a venue that's already set up and organised to handle it.

So where?

The location objective in terms of "green" weddings is to try to ensure that the wedding reception takes place either at the same venue as that of the ceremony, or failing that pretty close. In addition, a green wedding will be held at a location that's within the shortest possible travel distance for as many guests as possible.

This may rule out your long-held fantasy of getting married in a church on a remote Scottish hillside no matter how eco-friendly that is — especially if you, your family and friends all live in Birmingham. However let's not be total killjoys. If that's what you've set your heart on yet you can't bring yourself to disrupt the environment to shuttle everyone up there, get married locally in a registry office and afterwards go up to your church on the Scottish hillside for a blessing — just the two of you, and preferably by public transport.

Religious wedding

If you are having a religious wedding, to an extent your choice of venue becomes much narrower, as you may well choose to be married in a specific church, synagogue, mosque, temple or other religious building and/or by a specific religious celebrant. Try if you can to select a venue for the ensuing reception that is within walking distance of the ceremony venue. If it's too far, consider organising a "park and ride" system for your guests so they travel independently to a given point at the beginning of the day, then get taken to ceremony and reception — and back — by coach or minibus. (See Chapter 13.)

Local economy

Especially with all the controversy that's springing up now about just what really is green and what isn't we probably shouldn't agonise over whether three 15-seater minibuses are going to create more pollution than one 45-seater coach, or whether the reception is 100 yards from the ceremony or half a mile. What does make a difference is in containing the entire event within as small a geographical area as possible, and also in making the best use of local businesses and local produce. Not only does that keep transport and associated pollution down, but also helps keep alive the local economy.

Civil ceremony

If you're having a civil ceremony, the whole thing becomes much easier from an eco-friendly point of view, because in the UK now there is a wide choice of wedding locations which are licensed for marriages, many of which are suitable as reception venues, too. These range from commercial businesses to charitable foundations. For example:

- hotels
- restaurants
- leisure centres
- community centres
- country mansions
- historic buildings
- castles
- pavilions
- universities
- schools
- museums

Location

- islands
- barns
- oasthouses
- pumping stations
- mills
- mines
- quarries
- racecourses
- football clubs
- cricket clubs
- golf clubs
- breweries
- film and TV studios
- botanical gardens
- theme parks
- zoos
- theatres and cinemas
- the London Eye
- Tower Bridge
- Blackpool Tower
- airports
- railway stations
- trains

- ships

- submarines

- ... etc.

And that's not a complete list, by any means, especially as more and more venues are becoming available as time goes on. To find your choices, key "civil wedding venues" into your favourite search engine. There are several UK-based websites listing a good few thousand venues and they allow you to refine your search to a particular type and/or locality.

Greener choices?

Well, I suppose we had better rule out airports, to start with! But your primary criteria, as before, should be more about where and how big, rather than what, to minimise eco-damage. As I mentioned above, it's pointless choosing a venue that's very eco-friendly if it's miles away from where most of the guests are coming from. A good hotel or restaurant in a town that's within easy reach of everyone may not be as organic and may not even use only locally-sourced produce, but if it means avoiding 50 car journeys of 200 miles each, it may well be a better bet.

Business ethics

If the venue belongs to a large corporation — e.g. is one of many hotels in a chain — you may also want to consider how you feel about the business ethics of the parent company.

Catering

Next come the catering arrangements. Do the venue's caterers use only organic and locally sourced produce? Do they offer organic wine, preferably British, or if not can you bring your own? (See Chapters 10 and 11.) Can you bring in your own caterers of you want to? Do they operate a good recycling and composting setup? If it's a popular wedding venue, do they offer you the option of sharing floral arrangements and other decorations with couples immediately before and/or after you? (See Chapter 7.) If you're going to bring in your own suppliers, how easy is it for them to access the venue? How much travel will be involved for them?

Gardening

Another thing to bear in mind is that apparent beauty is often only skin deep in ecological terms. If you like the idea of having your wedding at a stunning country house hotel that offers all local produce from its own kitchen gardens and recycles all its wine bottles, you may like to consider how green they are with their gardening activities. That gorgeous, sweeping lawn may well have been treated with all kinds of noxious chemicals, weed killers, moss killers, etc., and be mowed almost every day by fuming petrol mowers. Even the vegetable garden may have been subjected to insecticides, weed killers, artificial fertilisers and various other things.

Weather

And before we leave the great outdoors, if you're getting married in the UK, think about the weather. Much as it may be splendid, romantic and environmentally desirable to tie the knot in the open air under the great sky above, it won't be much of an occasion if it's raining. By all means seek an outdoor venue, but ensure that the ceremony and reception can be brought in under cover should the weather decide not to play ball.

As with everything else, making the greenest wedding location choice is about getting a good balance. Unless you go to ridiculous extremes, there will be some elements of your location choice that are probably as not as green as they could be. But if you ensure that there is a reasonable balance of eco-friendly measures you can go ahead and create a stylish, enjoyable wedding — with no guilt.

Location

What you can do

- Avoid choosing a location abroad, even if you're combining wedding and honeymoon.

- Pick a location that's easily accessed by the majority of your guests.

- Organise a "park & ride" arrangement for guests, especially if the location is far from home.

- Pick a location that's easily accessed by public transport.

- Choose a reception location within as short a distance as possible of the ceremony location.

- Think twice about having your reception at home if you have to bring in all facilities.

- If having a civil wedding, arrange ceremony and reception in same location.

- Ensure reception location has a proper recycling policy.

- Ensure reception location catering uses local, preferably organic produce.

- See if you can "double up" with other couples getting married at around the same time, for things like flowers and decorations.

4 Stationery and Communications

This is a key area of your wedding where you can make quite a signifi-cant impact on **energy saving**, depending on how far you want to go.

The conventional route for invitations and other wedding stationery has been printed paper and card which are now known to involve a number of undesirable effects on the environment. Let's take a brief look at those, plus their greener alternatives.

Paper

A large percentage of paper made now is still of the "virgin" kind, and although recycled paper is becoming more widespread it nonetheless has some way to go. We've been hearing about "save the trees" for some years now, but every year we lose more than 40 million acres of forest worldwide despite vigorous replanting schemes. In the USA, some say that less than 5% of their original forests remain, and around 75% of the world's older-growth forests have been chopped down – with most of that having happened since the 1970s. Many such forests have quite simply been flattened, leaving the topsoil to erode away and wildlife to try to find another home.

As if that weren't bad enough, making paper out of those trees gobbles up masses of power and water, as well as involving the use of chemicals for bleaching and other purposes – one of the end results of which is the potential release of a nasty substance called dioxin which many experts claim can cause cancer.

Recycling paper

Recycling paper doesn't solve all these ecological problems, but it certainly helps. For starters, the process means that any unpleasant chemicals left behind from the paper's original printing process can be isolated and got rid of properly, rather than letting the chemicals wander out into the environment via conventional disposal. And of course recycling paper uses rather less in the way of energy, water and chemicals, not to mention the saving of trees.

Tree-free paper

One somewhat eco-friendlier way of making paper is becoming popular again – the tree-free variety. Interestingly enough this is hardly new; historical sources tell us that before the mid-nineteenth century the majority of paper was made not from tree fibre, but that of cotton and other plants. It was only later that century, when the whole logging and wood pulping industry really took off, that wood became the preferred material.

Today, plants used for tree-free paper include straw from grains like rye and wheat, plus specifically grown crops like industrial hemp and kenaf. Kenaf, particularly, offers a very high yield of fibre and grows quickly, so making it a very easily renewable source. Also, it doesn't need to be sprayed with insecticides to grow healthily.

Industrial hemp, too, is popular around the world with the exception of the USA, which banned it in the 1930s. This is not entirely unconnected with industrial hemp's proper name, which is *Cannabis sativa!* However we are assured that the hemp used for industrial purposes contains a mere fraction of the psychoactive chemical found in the *cannabis sativa* subspecies used for the illegal recreational drug.

Bamboo

Bamboo has been cited as another good source of fibre for papermaking and grows at an alarming speed. Some experts quote bamboo springing up at the rate of about 27 centimetres *per day*, with bamboos achieving a height of 20 metres or so and a circumference of about 20 centimetres per stem within one growing season of *just two months*. Even if these are slight exaggerations, bamboo would certainly seem to be a whole lot more renewable than trees. However, there is some controversy over the processing – presumably, involving chemicals – required to make bamboo into paper. It appears to need much more for much longer than for softer plants, so reducing its attractiveness in overall environmental terms.

Various other materials are said to be used for making alternative paper, including such intriguing ideas as dung, denim and even recycled paper money.

Printing

Conventional printing is yet another process that involves a motley crew of chemicals and unpleasant waste materials. Ink tends to be mineral oil based – i.e. related to petroleum – and some pigments in inks incorporate heavy metals. Waste can include anything from paper itself, to chemicals, water and power. And if a conventional photographic method is combined in with the printing, you get an additional menu of chemicals floating around threatening to pollute us (see Chapter 12).

Fortunately, more and more printing companies today are going "green". Realistically they can't be expected to eliminate all potentially polluting substances, but most are doing what they can to reduce the amount and nature of pollution created. Vegetable-based inks, rather than petroleum-based, are chosen and chemicals used by the printing presses are minimised. Both of these factors reduce emissions leading to less ozone damage and healthier working conditions for staff.

Digital printing is somewhat friendlier to the environment than old-fashioned conventional printing, and there are now eco-friendly toners available for digital printing systems to use which reduce greenhouse gas and sulphur dioxide emissions by a significant percentage.

To find green printers in your area, key "green printing" into your favourite search engine.

So what should we choose?

If you are determined to go the **printed paper** route, the greenest option is as follows:

1. Ensure all paper and card used is recycled.

2. Use only a green printing company.

3. Minimise the number of paper/card items you use.

I've gone into detail about points 1 and 2 earlier in this chapter, but point 3 is worth taking a closer look at. Possibly because printers and wedding stationery companies have a vested interest in selling you as many different items of wedding stationery as they can, you'll often find you end up with a large number of bits and pieces — some of which aren't necessary.

Let's look at some of the options: here is a list I've just compiled from various businesses offering wedding stationery services. All involve paper, and most involve either standard or personalised printing as well.

- Acceptance cards
- Bridal note paper
- Coasters
- Favour wraps
- Favour boxes

- Invitations – ceremony
- Invitations – reception
- Invitations – evening
- Order of the Day cards
- Order of Service cards
- Order of Ceremony cards
- Match books
- Menus
- Napkins
- Notepads
- Place cards
- Regrets cards
- Reply cards
- Save the date cards
- Table name cards or signs
- Table plans
- Thank you cards
- Thank you scrolls

... and don't forget the other inserts you'll often see enclosed with wedding invitations which include:

- Wedding lists
- Map of how to get to ceremony

- Map of how to get to reception

- List of hotels in the area

- List of local taxi companies

- List of train times, flights, etc

Now. How many of those do you need? Really? And especially if you do as much of your wedding communications via the internet as possible? Read on ...

If you want to be green, go "e"

The purists amongst us will squawk about the electricity needed to power the whole of the internet and okay, that's a point, especially as much electricity today is still generated by non-renewable energy.

However, if you compare the small amount of electricity required to send and receive your wedding communications online, with the ravages caused to old-growth forests around the world and noxious substances that lurk in the environment as a results of papermaking, printing, etc., I'd say there's no contest.

Email

This is the simplest form of communication and has the advantage of being very quick, easy to operate and is very low-cost.

With the exception of the elderly (most, but not all of them by any means) and any friends or relatives of yours who happen to live up a tree in a distant jungle, there are few people these days who do not have access to the internet either at home, at work, or both. Even in the case of those who do not own a computer at home and either don't go out to work or do not have work-based internet connections, usually there is a friendly relative or neighbour who can act as a go-between. (And for the odd one or two who simply cannot get it together, hand-written letters or phone calls should be acceptable alternatives.)

Bearing this in mind, most of your wedding communications can be done just using **email alone**. In fact there are companies today offering off-the-shelf or bespoke specially designed eWedding invitations – or "e-vites" – just for that purpose. To find these, key "email wedding invitations" or "e-vites" into your favourite search engine.

Although an email wedding invitation might raise an eyebrow or two amongst the more traditionally minded of your guests-to-be, once they know you are using email in order to make your wedding greener they should not be offended in any way. After all, since the turn of the twenty-first century eCards at Christmas, Hanukkah, birthdays and other special occasions have, increasingly, been replacing printed/posted cards with people not only doing it to save the planet, but also to save on cost. A number of people who send eCards at Christmas say they donate what they would have paid for printed cards and postage to charity, which is something you could consider for your wedding invitations, too.

What can be emailed?

Let's see how many of those printed wedding stationery items could be transferred to email:

Acceptance cards

These can easily be replaced by an email reply, telephone phone call or text message.

Bridal note paper

This is not necessary if you're using email. If you're good at online design or have a friend who is, you might be able to have a special "online wedding stationery" template made just for your online wedding correspondence, thank you emails, etc.

Coasters

Do you really need coasters?

Favour wraps

This depends entirely on the favour. If you choose these wisely it may not be necessary to wrap them up — they may come in their own packaging anyway, or you can simply add a bow or dried flower for decoration. See Chapter 9 for ideas.

Favour boxes

See favour wraps.

Invitations – ceremony

Replace these either with an ordinary email, or an "e-vite". Email also makes it easy to separate out guests for whichever part of your wedding you want them to attend, purely by compiling a list for each category.

Invitations – reception

See invitations — ceremony.

Invitations – evening

See invitations — ceremony.

Order of the Day cards

These can be replaced easily by email, being sent out to your final list a few days before the wedding.

Order of Service cards

Okay, maybe not. In theory you could email these as attachments to your guests so they could print them out and bring them on the day, but that probably is taking things too far and anyway involves printing on paper. If you need these (for a religious service) you can get them printed by a green printing company on to recycled paper or card.

Order of Ceremony cards

See Order of Service cards.

List of hotels in the area

This is easily replaced by email, as an attachment or in the body of the email itself.

List of local taxi companies

This is easily replaced by email, as an attachment or in the body of the email itself.

List of train times, flights, etc

This is easily replaced by email, as an attachment or in the body of the email itself.

Map of how to get to ceremony

This is easily replaced by email, as an attachment, or you could simply give guests the URL of an online map for them to study and/or print off if they want to. Failing that all they really need is the postcode and the address of the wedding and they can locate it themselves either on the web or via in-car satnav systems.

Map of how to get to reception

As for map to ceremony.

Match books

Don't worry about these now that the anti-smoking laws have come in here in the UK — they won't be needed!

Menus

No, these will probably have to be printed if you want them to be seen at the reception dinner. However, you don't need to have one done for each guest — one large menu on a card will do for each table. If you or someone close is good at handwriting, you could probably get them to create the menus on recycled card, which cuts down on printing and production problems. Don't forget, though, that email is a very useful way of finding out who can eat what, and offering a choice of, say, meat, fish, and vegetarian options well before the wedding so you can plan your catering efficiently.

Napkins

Nope, can't email these! Ideally they should be reusable cloth napkins, but realistically you may need to resort to the paper variety. Just make sure they get recycled afterwards.

Notepads

Not necessary, either by email or not.

Place cards

Once again in theory you could email seating plans to guests before the wedding. But people being what they are, half or more will forget where they're supposed to sit and if you're not careful the run-up to the dinner will be chaotic. Once again, call upon a calligrapher friend (or someone whose handwriting is good) and get them to write prettily on recycled card.

Regrets cards

Would you believe, these are sometimes enclosed within a fat invitation package so invitees can choose either this one or the acceptance card to send back as their answer. Email replaces the need for any of these wasteful variants.

Reply cards

See Regrets cards

Save the date cards

More popular in the USA than in the UK, these cards are sometimes used as a precursor to the wedding invitation (as soon as the date is set) to ensure key guests don't book themselves elsewhere on the day. I would have thought these could be replaced very satisfactorily by email or telephone calls.

Table name cards or signs

Once again, not possible to email, but a job for your calligrapher friend, on recycled card.

Table plans

See Place cards.

Thank you cards

These can be replaced by email as long as you make it clear that this is being done to be more eco-friendly. However, in some cases you may want to resort to an old fashioned handwritten note or card, particularly where the recipient is an older person who has grown up with more traditional ideas. Such cards or letters do not have to be specially printed, and you can use recycled paper or card for the purpose.

Thank you scrolls

These are an American idea which is being exploited in the UK by some wedding stationery companies. They are printed messages about your wedding to which you add your own personal thank you. To me though, they are particularly wasteful — I think most gift-giving guests would prefer a personal email or note.

Wedding lists

In Chapter 6 you'll see that a great many wedding list options are now available online, so rather than send an actual list by email you may well decided to give guests a URL to click on. If you do go for an actual list, though, it's easy enough to incorporate this into the body of an email via "cut and paste", or to attach it as a separate document.

Wedding websites

Wedding websites are increasingly popular, and deservedly so. They offer you the chance to centralise all your communications, share pictures and (usually) video footage of the events, update everyone involved on latest news, and generally act as base from which to plan the whole event.

The cost of this — and the duration (i.e. for how long the site is live) — varies from free, to around the £300 mark at the time of writing for a duration of two years or more. You can find what's available by keying "personal wedding websites" into your favourite search engine. You will also find some by keying in "wedding websites", but as these keywords can also refer to websites selling wedding services you might find it tedious to weed out those you don't want to look at.

You can, of course "DIY" your wedding website using one of the services available on the internet. To find these, key "make your own website" into your favourite search engine. Some are quite inexpensive but you will need to do cost comparisons yourself, as what is current at the time of writing may well be wildly out of date by the time you read this.

You may find it preferable to go with an organisation that is already set up to create wedding websites and take advantage of their established and proven facilities.

Whichever type you go for, the range of possibilities with a wedding website is huge. Obviously it won't replace any written or email communications or stationery altogether, but what it does is to offer the means to communicate far more information and images than would be practical either by conventional "snail mail" or even by email.

Here's a list of pages or sections you can include on a wedding website:

- Welcome
- Our story — how we met
- Our families
- Our engagement party (photographs, video)
- Our wedding list

- Hen celebration (photographs, video)
- Stag celebration (photographs, video)
- Wedding ceremony details
- Wedding reception details
- Online RSVP
- Message board
- Wedding menu (can include interactive choice)
- How to get there
- Where to stay
- Things to do in our area
- Our wedding ceremony (photographs, video)
- Our reception (photographs, video)
- Informal pictures (photographs and video taken by guests)
- Our honeymoon (photographs, video)

...etc.

In addition, of course, in many cases there is the option to set up a facility to show the wedding ceremony live on the site as a webcast, so distant relatives and friends can share the experience. This is a relatively eco-friendly thing to do (especially if it reduces long distance air travel) — but at the time of writing at least it can also be rather costly to set up, so be warned. You'll find more information on this by keying "wedding webcast" into your favourite search engine.

Whatever option you choose, it makes sense to ensure that access to your wedding website is password protected, to lessen the chances of receiving a thousand and one emails offering you every wedding service under the sun! What this means is that the people whom you want to access the site must sign in with their username/email address and a password. This should be offered to you by a wedding website provider, but if you opt for the DIY website option try to ensure the facility is incorporated here too.

Stationery and communications

What you can do

- Ensure all stationery is done by a "green" printer.

- Ensure that inks used are eco-friendly, i.e. vegetable, not mineral based.

- Ensure all paper and card used is recycled.

- Consider using "tree-free" paper made from other plants.

- Keep different elements of printed stationery and paper to a minimum.

- Replace as many printed elements as you can with email communications.

- Set up a wedding website and drive all communications through that.

5 Clothing and Cosmetics

For most women probably the most important element of planning their wedding is their choice of wedding dress and the bridesmaids' outfits. Traditionally, **your dress** is likely to be the most expensive item of clothing you will ever buy. And yet you will wear it only once, albeit on the most important day of your life. The same often goes for the bridesmaids and their outfits.

While many brides say "so be it, it's worth being extravagant on my wedding day", increasingly others are starting to scratch their heads and wonder how on earth any responsible person can spend thousands on wedding and bridesmaids' dresses when that money could be spent so much more usefully elsewhere.

And it's not just the money, although that matters a lot. It's also the waste of resources, fabric, energy, etc. ... often, the use of sweatshop manufacturing ... non-organic fabrics whose production pollutes the planet with toxic chemicals and whose workers suffer from poor pay as well ... the list goes on and on.

The good news is that there are many choices you can make that reduce the eco-problems caused by the production of traditional wedding dress and bridesmaids' outfits, without all of you having to wear biodegradable bin liners. In fact you could well end up with wedding outfits that are twice as beautiful and distinctive as any of those monotonous, multi-thousand "meringue" dresses you see worn by grinning "B" list actresses and their bridesmaids in the feelgood magazines. Being eco-friendly can and should be about creating style — only it's better, because it's style with a conscience.

Dry cleaning

You'll see in this chapter that I suggest various options of vintage, secondhand and other re-use of dresses, and in the majority of these cases you will need to get the dress dry cleaned. Unfortunately, the chemicals used in dry cleaning are highly toxic and when their vapour is released into the air, it contributes quite unpleasantly to the "hole in the ozone layer". At the same time there is a risk that dry cleaning chemicals get released into the water supply, causing pollution there too.

Many dry cleaners now claim to reuse/reprocess their solvent chemicals which helps a bit, and at the time of writing there are a number of companies in the UK offering different dry cleaning processes that are claimed to be much kinder to the environment. To find out more, key "eco-friendly dry cleaning" into your favourite search engine.

When buying new, consider seriously opting for washable fabrics.

Wedding dresses

I don't know about you, but when I got married the thought of squeezing myself into a tight bodiced strapless gown a size too small for me with several cubic metres of scratchy tulle around my ankles, then wearing it for at least 12 hours, made my skin crawl. My wedding being in December, instead I opted for a long sleeved ivory and gold brocade kaftan with matching headband, off the peg from a department store, which was elegant, simple and above all comfortable — and warm! Mind you that was a long time ago now and looking back, I dread to think where the fabric came from and how it was all made. And were I to do it all again, I would definitely be attracted to the natural fabrics and streamlined, elegant looks possible with the more eco-friendly choice of wedding gowns we have now.

Natural fabrics

One relatively eco-friendly option is to have your dress made by a local dressmaker using natural fabrics from fairtrade sources. Ideally, the fabric should have been produced locally too — keeping everything local, as we know, forms a significant part eco-consumerism. However realistically, not many natural fibres are grown in the UK, which means such fabrics will have been imported. If you're concerned about the transport pollution element, you may prefer to buy a secondhand wedding dress and have that remodelled by your dressmaker. More of that later.

If you want to use natural fabrics your choice is still quite wide. Natural, renewable options — made in fairtrade conditions — include cotton, linen, wool, silk (kind to silkworms, too), hemp, cashmere, and even bamboo. You also may want to ensure that natural dyes have been used. For current suppliers of eco-friendly and fairtrade fabrics, key "natural fabrics" into your favourite search engine.

Re-usability

Another sensible element to build into the design and making of your wedding dress is one of re-usability. So many women spend fortunes on a wedding dress only for it to sit in mothballs for the next 30 years, sadly going to waste, because it's inappropriate to be worn anywhere else. Of course there are eco-friendly alternatives to that — see below — but why not factor in the possibility of having the dress altered into a stunning evening or cocktail dress for yourself later on? You could leave it in its original colour, or have it dyed using natural dyes. And each time you wear it in the future, it will remind you of your terrific wedding day!

Pure white

Whatever the fabric you use, try to avoid pure white. That's because it is likely to have been bleached using strong chemicals which are potentially harmful.

Secondhand

Buying secondhand is another useful option. Long gone are the days when it wasn't "cool" to be seen looking around charity and other secondhand shops. Today they're havens of wonderful treasures, many of which can be bought very reasonably. If you hunt around you'll find a number of outlets selling secondhand wedding dresses — you'll see a good selection online by keying "secondhand wedding dresses" into your favourite search engine. You may also find some excellent bargains on eBay. Some of these dresses will be new, too — manufacturers often sell off "seconds" with slight imperfections to the commercial secondhand businesses, or donate them to the charity stores. Any imperfection you find on a dress can usually be put right by a clever dressmaker, and might even be so slight that no-one other than a strict quality controller would notice it — so it can be ignored.

Oxfam

In recent times the charity Oxfam has enjoyed a huge success with its specialist secondhand bridal shops in the UK. These shops specialise not only in secondhand wedding dresses but also bridesmaids' dresses, and even outfits for mothers of the bride and groom. At the time of writing these Oxfam bridal shops are based in the following locations in the UK:

- Bracknell (Berks)
- Bradford
- Cambridge
- Chippenham (Wiltshire)
- Coventry
- Eastbourne
- Heswall (Wirral)
- Leicester
- Poole (Dorset)
- Southampton

As these first 10 outlets have been so successful, with luck by the time you read this there will be more specialist Oxfam bridal shops available for you to check out elsewhere.

Once you have your secondhand dress, you may then need to ask a friend or professional dressmaker to alter it. Again, try to keep this as local as possible to ensure the minimum of travelling around.

Hire

It's also possible to hire your wedding dress from one of a number of companies which you'll find either in Yellow Pages or by keying "wedding dress hire" into your favourite search engine. Here, there will be quite a heavy dry cleaning implication because the dress will be cleaned each time it is returned to the hire company, and you will have no control over how that's done. However, at least the dress will be well recycled!

Borrowing

Borrowing a dress is another helpful option – from a friend, colleague or relative – and you could even consider **sharing a dress** with another bride-to-be, perhaps involving some alterations or changing of trim, detail, etc. to ensure each bride's individuality. Some wedding dresses, like christening dresses, have been in families for generations and become a precious piece of family history. It may well be worth your while exploring your female relatives' attics to see what treasures you can find.

And after your wedding?

If you want to be green, don't pack your dress away forever! If you have opted for the remodelling idea – having the dress remade into an evening or cocktail dress, possibly dyed – then do it ... don't put it off, or you may never get around to it. If you haven't made that selection, then offer it on loan to other brides, sell it on eBay or to a secondhand shop, or donate it to the charity shop of your choice.

Veils and headpieces

If you are to have a veil, you should ensure that it's made from silk tulle, and not from nylon or other artificial fabric which will only clog up the environment once finished with. If you're having your veil made, rather than buying ready-made, try to get that done by a local supplier.

Of course you may prefer to find an antique or vintage veil from a secondhand shop, or borrow a veil from a friend or family member. Like wedding dresses, veils are often handed down from one generation to the next.

If you want to wear a **tiara**, you should be able to hire one from a bridal shop, rather than go to the expense of buying one. Obviously not many of us are likely to wear tiaras made from real gemstones and precious metals, and those of us who do are likely to be loaned family heirlooms.

Perhaps a greener option all round, though, is to forgo the veil and instead adorn you hair with real or fabric flowers, or a piece of jewellery.

Jewellery

In Chapter 1 I went into a lot of detail about the issues surrounding real diamonds, coloured gemstones and precious metals, so I won't repeat myself here.

However, be aware of these issues when contemplating buying new jewellery for the bride and bridesmaids, and if possible select pieces of imitation stones and metals which have been made in fairtrade conditions.

Be warned; much of the **very cheap cubic zirconium and silver or platinum/rhodium/etc plated jewellery** on sale in the UK at the time of writing, at least, is made in faraway countries where the pay and conditions of labour are dubious to put it mildly — hence UK retailers being able to sell real silver and CZ for a few pounds per item and still make a profit. You may feel it's better to pay a bit more, but know the makers of the jewellery were not children and got a fair wage.

Shoes

Much as we may want to ensure our entire wedding outfits are brand, spanking new to match our brand, spanking new life, there are no rules which say you have to buy new shoes. In fact if anything, **new shoes are a bad idea**. Why? Because on your wedding day you're going to be on your feet for many hours, and possibly dancing the night away too. The last thing you need is pinching shoes that make your feet hurt and with the best will in the world, new shoes can be uncomfortable when you first wear them.

If you happen to own a pair of dressy shoes that will go with your dress, and they're comfortable, you will probably find yourself enjoying your day even more wearing those, than you would in new shoes. If you don't have any suitable shoes though, there are still some options that are greener than buying new from a High Street store.

Charity shops and other secondhand outlets are usually very good sources of not just secondhand, but also new or **nearly-new shoes**.

Frequently people will buy a pair of shoes in a sale or on a whim and never wear them, or at least only wear them once. If they don't fit properly or the owner dislikes them they will often be the first things to be chucked out and sent to the charity shop. How do I know? Because I have done that myself, many times! The result, though, is that you can pick up some excellent bargains that way and the shoes have a new, or at least recycled, opportunity in life.

If you are going to buy new, you may want to consider more ethical choices which have been made using vegetable dye, manufactured in fairtrade conditions, and non-leather options like natural fibres. To find more on this, key "ethical footwear" into your favourite search engine.

Lastly, whether you're buying new or secondhand, try if you can to select a design and colour that you will wear again after the wedding. White fabric shoes can be dyed another colour, yes, but sometimes — especially with vegetable dyes — the colours can run a bit and in any case if there is any staining on the shoe before it's dyed, the new colour might be uneven. A pretty design in, say, pastel colours will look great with dressy and/or summery outfits for some time after the wedding day, and will look equally lovely with your wedding outfit — especially if the colour picks up on your choice of contrasting colour.

Lingerie

Yes, you can get eco-friendly underwear! Usually it's made from hemp, fairtrade cotton and other natural fabrics. You can even buy eco-friendly bras made from fairtrade cotton, with bamboo under wiring.

To find more, key "ethical lingerie" into your favourite search engine.

Bridesmaids' dresses

Another very heavy expense in the traditional wedding is that of the bridesmaids' dresses, whether the bride pays for them or the bridesmaids pick up the cost themselves. When you consider that many bridesmaids' dresses are entirely unsuitable for the bridesmaids to wear afterwards as evening or cocktail dresses – and anyway are not necessarily to their taste in design – the whole exercise looks almost as wasteful as the "meringue" wedding dress that costs thousands and only gets worn once.

People often recommend that you should select a colour, then let the bridesmaids choose the design of their dress themselves. Certainly this opens up the potential for using their dresses after your wedding. However, rather than dictate the colour yourself, which might not be to their liking, it might be more democratic – and practical – if you choose a colour together with your bridesmaids and agree on one that everyone likes ... and will wear later.

The other side of the same coin is to determine one particular design of bridesmaid's dress, and then let your bridesmaids choose their preferred colour. You can then co-ordinate the theme by getting them to wear identical shawls, pashminas, stoles or sashes.

If you don't want to go down the "new" route, it is possible to **rent bridesmaids' dresses** from wedding clothing hire companies. If you don't have any luck there, you might find that an ordinary dress hire shop can help by acquiring the same design or colour of appropriate evening or cocktail dresses for the correct number, in correct sizes.

Also, you will sometimes find bridesmaids' dresses in secondhand shops and charity shops.

Finally, unless your bridesmaids really do intend to wear their dresses after your wedding, encourage each one to donate her dress to a charity shop.

Children's clothes

Here you might not immediately see the point of buying clothes that can be worn again after your wedding as children grow out of things so fast, but bear in mind that **children's clothes do get recycled** quite a lot within families and groups of friends. So they can have a long shelf life.

The fashion for little boys in sailor suits and little girls in mini-"meringues" seems to have passed, thank heavens, because these days even a very young child wouldn't be seen dead by his or her peers in such unreal costumes. So you can take it as a certainty that outfits like that will never be worn again, unless perhaps by someone buying them for another wedding from a secondhand shop.

More practical and appreciated all round is the type of outfit which can be dressed up with coloured sashes, bows, frills, etc., but once those accoutrements are stripped off, consists of clothes the children can wear later without embarrassment. That will have a domino effect when the clothes get handed down, too.

It makes a lot of sense to ensure all fabrics involved in the **children's clothing are washable**, not only from an eco-friendly but also a practical point of view. Children's clothes get dirty very quickly — even while being tried on before your wedding they could suffer a splodge of chocolate or a smear of colouring pencil. And if the clothes are to be used afterwards, easily washable fabrics will earn you brownie points with the parents as well as with the planet.

One last tip about children's wedding outfits which is not really relevant to eco-friendliness but is important nonetheless, is to **make sure the clothes will fit *on the day***, not necessarily when the clothes are bought or made. Brides — especially if they haven't had any children yet — often overlook the fact that children grow extremely fast and clothes that fit on Day 1 will probably be tight by Day 60 and ridiculously outgrown by Day 200 or so. If you are getting the children's clothes well in advance of the wedding, ensure you choose one or even two sizes larger than that which fits them now. Probably, it's worth waiting until fairly close to the day to get the children's outfits if you can, although even two or three weeks can make a difference. When in doubt, get the next size up.

Groom, best man, ushers

With clothes for the groom, best man and ushers, in many cases the traditional route of hiring morning suits, tuxedos or other outfits has been an eco-friendly option for some years now. Unless your groom and his friends are regular and frequent wedding-goers/formal socialisers they are unlikely to want to own such clothing, so going to the **local wedding gear hire shop** is the logical step for them.

However, hiring men's wedding clothes can be expensive, and some couples may prefer to get the men dressed in their own, conventional dark suits and simply supply co-ordinating accessories like ties, cravats, cummerbunds, buttonholes, etc.

If you should consider buying new, though, you may want to pursue a greener approach buy ensuring that all fabrics are natural, fairtrade-produced and preferably are washable.

Cosmetics

There really isn't a great deal to say about cosmetics for your wedding without going into the whole issue of how cosmetics in our modern world can be full of chemicals not only damaging to the planet, but to you, too. And yet cosmetics play a relatively small part in your wedding preparations.

But do they? Really? Many brides treat themselves – and quite rightly – to facials, beauty treatments, hair treatments, etc., and also involve their bridesmaids in similar activities. Often, the "hen night" or "hen party" is devoted to such activities. (See Chapter 2.)

Now whereas more and more venues offering such treatments are using organic and planet-friendly cosmetics and methods, there is still quite a way to go in terms of cleaning up the cosmetic industry.

According to my research, at the time of writing, in the UK, any product that contains a weeny "at least" 1% of ingredients which can be obtained from nature, can call itself "natural". Wow. Impressive, huh? Especially when you consider what awful substances may be lurking within the other 98–99%.

Intriguingly, currently the only "cosmetic" product which can be certified (or not) by the UK Soil Association, is toothpaste. We should hope that the Soil Association's remit will grow substantially in the future, but that is unlikely to happen overnight. To check this out go to: http://www.soilassociation.org.

In the meantime, here are a few thoughts that might influence your choice of cosmetic and hair care for you and your bridesmaids ....

Additives

Many commercially produced cosmetics contain a cocktail involving some of the following:

- Formaldehyde
- Fragrance
- Imidazolidinyl urea
- Isopropyl alcohol
- Methyl paraben
- Paraffin
- Propylene glycol
- Sodium lauryl sulphate

Other additives, on the other hand, may not be as nasty as their official titles suggest, e.g.:

- Ascorbic acid (vitamin C)
- Grapefruit seed extract
- Potassium sorbate
- Sorbic acid
- Tocopherol (vitamin E)
- Retinol (vitamin A)

What harm can the potentially nasty ones create, you may wonder. In small doses, not much, perhaps. But when planning your wedding, it may be of interest to you to consider these threats and warn those closely involved with your day to avoid them.

Hair

Hair products, too, can be frightening.

One of the web addresses I researched for this book talked of the poster's mother, who sprayed her hair every day with commercial hairspray and died of kidney failure — which the poster blamed on his mum's inhalation of the hairspray — aged just 51. My own mother, who wore her hair in a (pinned) upswept style for 40 years or more and sprayed it every day (sometimes twice a day) with commercial hair spray, died of lung cancer aged 82 despite never having smoked a single cigarette. She was convinced that inhaling the aerosol hairspray was responsible.

Potentially unpleasant substances in hair spray include at least six chemicals which are known to be dangerous. Six chemicals in hair wax are thought to be damaging, too, as are a further 12 in hair gel, and a further eight in hair mousse.

For further information on this, key "natural hair care" into your favourite search engine.

So what do you do if you want to be green with your use of cosmetics in the run-up to, and on, your wedding day?

Be realistic. No matter how green we want to be, there will be times — especially now — when it may just not be an option where cosmetics are concerned.

However, there's nothing to stop you, your groom, your wedding party and your friends having a good think about cosmetics, and perhaps readjusting your views about them for the future. And your wedding might just be a good time for that "think" to happen.

Clothing and cosmetics

What you can do

- Ask yourself if this really should be the splash-out of your life, or could you be greener?

- Ensure that any dry cleaning involved is kept to a minimum.

- Try, if you can, to ensure any dry cleaning uses the most recent eco-friendly techniques.

- If buying new, try to choose local suppliers and natural fabrics.

- See if you can create a wedding dress that could be remodelled for future use.

- Avoid fabrics that are pure white, because they may have been bleached using toxic chemicals.

- Consider buying secondhand wedding, bridesmaids' and even "mothers'" outfits.

- Also consider hiring wedding and bridesmaids' dresses.

- Could you borrow a dress? Think about that.

- After your wedding, should you not want to wear your dress again, donate it.

- Try to use a veil and/or head dress that is an heirloom.

- Find a veil and head dress in an antique or vintage store.

- Hire a tiara from a wedding store rather than buy one, or use a family heirloom.

- Choose jewellery that conforms with what I've outlined in this chapter and in Chapter 1.

- Consider avoiding new shoes and going for something used ... whether by you or someone else.

- If you really want to make a difference, consider eco-friendly lingerie too.

- Use your common sense to help bridesmaids wear dresses they can use again.

- Consider hiring bridesmaids' outfits from ordinary evening/dress-wear outlets.

- Consider buying bridesmaids' outfits from charity shops.

- Ensure that children's clothes will fit them on the day.

- See that children's clothes can be worn again not only by your child attendants, but also by the children to whom those clothes might be handed down.

- Consider whether the guys should hire suits, or maybe wear their own with some co-ordinating accessories?

- Consider what damage current cosmetics might be doing to your skin, and perhaps look into more sensitive, natural beauty treatments.

6 Gifts

With our awareness of and concern about the environment growing at such a fast pace, it's not surprising that profit-minded entrepreneurs are popping out of the woodwork everywhere to cash in on the eco-friendly market — especially for gifts. They come in all shapes and sizes — organic, fairtrade, cruelty-free, natural, sustainable, recycled, handmade, ethical, reusable, reclaimed, chemical-free, biodegradable, energy-efficient, you name it — and consist of almost every type of gift item you can think of from kettles to chunks of rain forest. Just key "eco-friendly gifts" into your favourite search engine to find out how many permutations there are, from the sensible to the silly.

While I'm not suggesting there is anything dishonest going on here, nonetheless you may begin to wonder just what sort of wedding gifts you can ask for that really are going to be eco-friendly — but will not cost your wedding guests small fortunes to buy purely because there are eco-friendly labels attached.

Gifts for yourselves

If you and your intended genuinely do need to set up home properly there is absolutely nothing to feel guilty about if you ask your guests to make a selection from a (green) wedding list. Although in theory it may be more eco-friendly not to throw out that 20-year-old sofa with saggy springs and continue to use it for another 20 years, the reality is that getting your friends to contribute towards a new one that's handmade by local craftspeople is probably just as green and a damned sight more comfortable and realistic. (Especially if you donate the old sofa to a good cause or dispose of it via an organisation like Freecycle: http://www.freecycle.org.) And that's before you consider the benefits to your comfort and posture.

In any case, whether you need to set up home with new things or not, your friends and family are going to want to do something to mark this very special occasion, so you may as well make use of it if you need it.

Money

Asking guests to give money is usually seen as not very PC, but if you think about it, it's actually quite green. Money can be sent via electronic methods — even by PayPal or similar service to your wedding website (see Chapter 4) — which creates virtually no pollution, uses no resources other than a bit of electricity, and puts the responsibility for buying green items entirely into your hands.

Older guests, in particular, might baulk at sending you money as a wedding present because historically it was seen as a rather tasteless thing to do. However, if you stress the point that **gifts of money can be a damned sight more eco-friendly** than almost any other type of gift, even the most diehard traditionalist should see sense.

Obviously, you will need to adhere to the traditional thank-you rules and tell each guest what you will be using the money for — either to buy a one-off item, to put towards a larger item, etc. — so they will not think you've blown it all on an exotic honeymoon!

Green wedding lists

At the time of writing, there are UK-based companies offering green wedding lists, whereby your guests can take their pick of recycled, sustainable, fairtrade and other gift options. There are not many of them at the moment and those that do exist have a fairly limited choice of items. These might include:

- recycled glassware
- fairtrade bed linen

- organic cotton bedding

- bamboo items and furniture

- kitchenware

- fairtrade and locally-made ceramics

- organic towels

- eco-friendly candles

... and so-on. In time I'm sure there will be companies both online and offline who will offer complete wedding list facilities covering everything you need to set up home with appropriately green products, so keep an eye on progress by keying "green wedding lists" or "good gifts" into your favourite search engine.

In the meantime, though, you may need to compile a green wedding list of your own, which you could post on your wedding website (see Chapter 4) with contact details and online links. You could use one of the existing green gift suppliers who currently offer wedding lists as a basis, and then add to it. Here are some ideas to get you thinking ...

Energy-efficient electrical goods

Most major manufacturers of anything from freezers to toasters are now much more conscious of the need to be energy efficient and new models are being produced that comply with this. The majority of new electrical goods and appliances must be clearly labelled with their energy efficiency rating so you know just how well they will perform. (Secondhand appliances are not required to be labelled this way, though.) Key "energy efficient electrical goods" into your favourite search engine.

Low energy lightbulbs

Not the most glamorous of wedding gifts but useful all the same! These bulbs are widely available from electrical stores, supermarkets and other retail outlets.

Environmentally friendly furniture

Ensure that any new furniture that goes on your wedding list is made from sustainable or reclaimed wood and other materials, and that upholstery is made with natural, fairtrade fabrics. Try if you can to specify locally made furniture, so supporting eco-consumerism. Key "eco-friendly furniture" into your favourite search engine.

Recycled glassware

A number of companies both online and offline offer ranges of very attractive glassware made from recycled glass. Obviously this includes various different forms of tumbler, wine glasses etc., plus vases, dishes, bowls, and so-on. Key "recycled glassware" into your favourite search engine.

Cookware

Some people say that stainless steel, coated metal and even aluminium pans and casseroles can be a problem as there is the possibility of substances leaching out into your food. Cast iron is said to be the greenest option. And because cast iron pots are so heavy you'll develop powerful muscles in your arms through using them! It's also sensible to choose good quality cookware because provided that you look after it, it should last for a very long time, unlike the cheaper materials.

Plastic kitchenware

Try if you can to suggest biodegradable plastics for kitchenware like washing up bowls, colanders, dish racks, etc. At the time of writing, there does not seem to be much on the market along these lines but such products may be available in the future. Ordinary plastic kitchenware is, at least, likely to be recyclable.

Locally made crockery

There are some very talented designers and manufacturers of ceramics and fine china in the UK, so it makes sense to ensure that any crockery items on your wedding list are made here and not imported. If you have a pottery or ceramics business in your neighbourhood, they might be prepared to create a set of crockery for you which would be a delightful addition to your list.

Cutlery

If you really want to be eco-friendly it's even possible to buy biodegradable cutlery! However, assuming you want to keep yours for as long as possible, you should avoid the potato starch and wooden options which will last for a very short time and instead look at perhaps — cutlery made out of recycled stainless steel, although that (see Cookware, above) may have its problems too. Your best bet is to key "eco-friendly cutlery" into your favourite search engine and check out the most recent developments.

Beds and bedding

Try if you can to include UK-made beds, preferably in sustainable or reclaimed wood, with mattresses made from natural, fairtrade substances. Biodegradable duvets and pillows exist at the time of writing but as far as I can see they are only available in North America. Interestingly enough they're made from a fabric derived from corn. Also available are organic sheets, blankets and other bedding in organic fair-trade cotton and fabric made from bamboo. Once again, these are primarily sold from North America but are certain to come to the UK before long. Key "organic bedding" or "eco-friendly bedding" into your favourite search engine.

Metalware

Silver and pewter are popular metals for wedding gifts, but as you'll have gathered if you read Chapter 1, metal mining is usually very "dirty" in environmental terms. Silver mining is every bit as disastrous as gold mining, and the process of silver plating usually involves a cocktail of nasty chemicals including acids. Pewter, being an alloy of tin, lead and sometimes other substances, may have some potential hazards too. Pewter made in the UK today has to be free from lead and nickel by law, but many pewter objets d'art (and silver/silver plated ones) are imported. In fact centuries ago, pewter was used widely for plates and bowls, before ceramics came into being, and people eating high-acid foods like tomatoes would sometimes succumb to lead poisoning ... the acid in the food would dissolve the lead in the pewter and bingo!

If you are happy to have silver, silver plate and pewter gifts, it might be greener to insist on secondhand or antique pieces which, at least, have made their contribution to environmental problems a long time ago and are unlikely to do any further harm. However, you may decide that you would prefer gifts of ornaments and tableware made out of greener sub-stances like recycled glass or sustainable/reclaimed wood.

Garden and plants

This range of essential household items does not appear on many wedding lists as it isn't perhaps as glamorous as are the satin sheets and crystal candlesticks, but unless you live in an apartment with no balcony or window boxes you're going to need a selection of these in a new home, and probably a top-up if you're living there already. Most local garden centres offer gift vouchers which your guests could purchase, or they could put on order their choice from your list of various organic house plants, outdoor plants, shrubs, trees, etc. that you can collect when you're ready to use them. Other options could include hand tools, electric hedge clippers, mower, strimmer, leaf blower, etc. (avoid petrol motor versions as they pump out awful fumes). Try if you can to ask for British made products rather than imports, even if they are a bit more expensive. Finally, don't forget to add to the list such items as a composter, bird feeders, and even a wormerie. Key "green gardening" into your favourite search engine.

DIY equipment

You may well want to include a drill, sander, saw and other power tools for home repairs, and these should be as energy-efficient as possible. You'll also need such humble items as a hammer, screw driver, spirit level and other such things which should, if possible, be British made.

Artworks

If there are some particular paintings and sculptures that you like, preferably created by local artists using natural, organic materials, there's no reason why they shouldn't go on your list — unless they're very expensive!

One final thought about wedding lists: it's greener to limit your range of stores involved to a few, or preferably one, from the point of view that transport of gifts from there to you will be minimised. On the other hand though, at the time of writing anyway, there are few stores in the UK which could offer you a sufficiently comprehensive green selection all from under one roof. You really need to make your decisions here based on your own particular circumstances.

Gifts for the planet

Often, a couple getting married will have more than enough of what they need to equip their home and the last thing they want to receive is yet another egg coddler or ironing board. If this sounds like you, there are some alternative things you can ask for that will make a useful contribution to the **environment** and/or to **charity**.

For starters, there is **your honeymoon** (see Chapter 14). Now, asking guests to contribute towards the cost of flying yourselves to the other side of the world for two weeks of unashamed luxury and self-indulgence is not the most green way of looking at things. However you may decide to go on an eco-tourism based trip, or perhaps even cross a desert or climb a mountain to raise money for charity.

There are numerous charities and other **good causes** that are delighted to receive donations from your guests. If you key "charity gift lists" into your favourite search engine you'll find a wide choice of interested organisations, and there are even specialised companies (operating online) who will set up a bespoke list consisting of the charities you choose and manage the list and donations for you. Among the many mainstream charitable organisations represented here, there are a great many green-influenced charities and projects you can include, with options like buying some seeds for an African farmer or providing some support for a rainforest community.

Gifts for attendants

Traditionally brides and grooms not only give each other personal gifts on their wedding day but also give keepsake gifts to bridesmaids, the best man, ushers, and child attendants.

If you want to keep this as green as possible, consider — for the girls, anyway — buying some pretty vintage or antique jewellery (some antique costume jewellery is lovely and not very expensive) is a good way to make your statement of gratitude without digging up new precious metals or stones. Alternatively, you may want to make them a gift of some organic, preferably locally produced toiletries, soaps, candles, skincare products, etc.

For the men, you may well find some attractive cufflinks in local antique and secondhand jewellery shops, or perhaps a smart secondhand fountain pen which can be used with eco-friendly ink.

Another alternative that often goes over well with either the girls or the guys is some tasty organic, preferably locally produced wine! British wines are no longer considered an expensive rarity. Many are organically produced and most are delicious. For more on this, see Chapter 11.

For the children, once again you might find suitable items in your local secondhand and antique jewellery shops. You may also want to find eco-friendly toys made out of sustainable/reclaimed wood, preferably by local craftspeople, or made from bioplastics which at the time of writing are available in the US and may well be available in the UK by the time you read this.

NB: I haven't included gifts for guests or wedding favours here, as I go into that in Chapter 9.

Gifts

What you can do

- Beware of the current boom in so-called green gifts in the light of potential commercial exploitation, and don't be afraid to sort out the wheat from the chaff.

- Don't be intimidated by pressure to be green — if you need practical gifts for your home, ask for them.

- Don't get carried away by excessive green ideas; at the end of the day you need to have a life, too.

- Gifts of money may not be PC, but can well be very green because it puts the choice of items entirely in your hands — furthermore, transferring money electronically is a pretty green way of doing it.

- By all means use a company that offers green wedding lists, but be aware that their choice of gifts may well be limited.

- Think carefully through what you need for your marital home and design your gift list appropriately, preferably managing it through your wedding website rather than by paper and post.

- If you don't need gifts and equipment for your home, consider asking for donations towards an environmentally productive honeymoon, or a honeymoon that involves your participation in a charitable activity abroad.

- And equally if you don't need gifts and equipment for your home, consider asking guests to give to charity and environmental projects instead.

- When choosing gifts for bridal attendants, choose recycled jewellery, organic products and for children, eco-friendly toys.

7 Flowers and Decorations

You could be forgiven for thinking that flowers and floral decorations, being "natural", are not a primary source of environmental concern. Sadly that's a long way from the truth. Many cut flowers are imported from hundreds or even thousands of miles away and because of their perishable nature, they come by air. The countries where they are grown are not always as fussy about use of pesticides and other chemicals as we are in this country, so pollution from that is a serious issue on top of the air travel problem.

In the US the picture is especially difficult. Many of the commercial floral products sold in the US are imported from South America where, in several places, pollution laws regarding horticulture are slack to put it mildly. Although fresh foods imported into the US are subject to certain anti-pollution regulations, flowers obviously are not considered to be food and so do not come under those guidelines. Consequently, many of the growers cheerfully spray and anoint away with toxic chemicals, vestiges of which not only can enter into the US on the flowers, but also lurk around in the countries of their origin, potentially leaching into the soil and contaminating it along with the water supply. In addition, it seems there is a very high rate of serious and sometimes fatal illnesses among the horticultural workers in some of the South American countries, which can be attributed directly to the chemical pollution.

All this may make you take a second look the next time you walk past a brilliant display of exotic blooms in your local flower shop, and certainly may make you want to reconsider the traditional floral decorations for your wedding. Happily, there are some alternatives that are much kinder to the planet.

Eco-friendlier flowers

A lot depends on when your wedding is to take place, but if it occurs at an appropriate time you should be able to source flowers locally, preferably grown organically. At the time of writing, there are very few organic florists in the UK. However there are many in North America and the likelihood is that, as concern in the UK about environmental issues continues to grow, more organic florists will start trading. To check on this, key "organic florists" into your favourite search engine.

If organic flowers aren't a realistic proposition you can still make a significant reduction in planet damage by using **locally grown flowers**, perhaps bought from a local farmer's market or nursery. This will mean you must use flowers that happen to be in season at the time of your wedding, but even so in the UK that still leaves you and your flower arranger with a good choice for the summer season, and also late spring and early autumn.

Some brides these days — especially in North America — are determined to **grow their own organic flowers** for their weddings. Obviously this assumes that they are planning many months in advance, but it's a lovely idea! If you are — or a close friend or relative is — a keen gardener with a decent sized garden or allotment, and your wedding is not due to take place for some time, that's an option you might like to consider.

One point that all environmental experts make is whatever you do, and however romantic it may seem to do so, do *not* pick and use **wild flowers** for your wedding. Wild flowers are precious enough as it is, with agriculturalists still savaging them with chemicals and developers chopping up their habitats to build houses, roads and factories. If we pick them, they do not have the opportunity to reseed themselves and eventually could disappear altogether. Another point about wild flowers, too: in the past, in my (then) ignorance, whenever I picked a few wild flowers out in the field to bring home and put in a vase of water, they would wilt within a couple of hours. (This hardly makes them suitable as cut flowers for wedding decorations.) It was almost as if they were getting back at me for having disturbed them. Needless to say I no longer do that, but enjoy them to the full when out in the countryside.

If you grow wild flowers yourself from seed, I suppose you can be excused! However bear in mind that these, too, will wilt quickly. Varieties of flowers with a lot more staying power are roses, carnations, gladioli, etc. If you fancy **growing your own** then check out which species are (a) feasible for you to grow, (b) in season at the time of your wedding, and (c) likely to last until the very end of your reception and perhaps even beyond. For more ideas, key "long lasting cut flowers" into your favourite search engine.

Working with florists

If you use a florist, even if they do use locally-grown, organic flowers or at least import fairtrade flowers, they may still use accessories which can be hard or even impossible to recycle. At the time of writing, the green foam used by florists in arrangements – often called "oasis" – is not recyclable. The same applies to some of the other things they use like packaging and preserving solutions.

You might also like to ask them about their own approach to eco-friendliness and particularly recycling and composting: do they donate still-usable arrangements to nursing homes and other deserving causes? Do they operate a sensible composting policy for flowers that really are past it, as well as all the trimmings and cast offs?

Finally, you may feel that although not all flowers used are local and/or organic, to use a florist local to your wedding venue makes a great deal of eco-sense. As always, it's about getting the balance right.

Doubling up

One way of conserving energy and minimising the use of flowers is to double up on the flowers used for your ceremony, with those used for the reception. Naturally if the ceremony and reception are held in the same place this is not a problem. However, even if the two venues are separate, sometimes it is possible to arrange for people to transfer the floral arrangements from the ceremony venue to the reception, while you and your guests are having photographs taken and getting the first glass or two of bubbly under your belts.

Another element of "doubling up" that can provide a greener solution is to consult other couples getting married at the same venue on the same day, and see if your flower arrangements and other decorations can be co-ordinated to avoid wastage.

Here's a quote from my last weddings book, *The A to Z of Wedding Worries ... and how to put them right ...*

What about the wedding before yours?

You will often find that churches and other places of worship as well as secular wedding venues get heavily booked up in the spring and summer months, with one wedding after another taking place on the same day.

This can present problems if you want to get yourself or your florist into the ceremony venue to do the flowers prior to your wedding.

One solution to this is to contact the other couples getting married on the same day in the same place, get together with them, agree on an floral scheme you all like, and share the cost. Not only will this solve the practical problem, but also it will save you all quite a lot of money.

That idea may save money and certainly will be greener. Think about it!

Bouquets and things

I know that upon the bride's bouquet hangs a whole load of tradition, not least of which is the bridesmaids' and other girls' burning desire to catch the bouquet as you throw it over your shoulder so they may be the next in your crowd to marry, but ...!! There is no reason why your bouquet should not consist of an eclectic mix of local, seasonal fresh delights. And if you want really to be eco-chic, consider – instead of a bouquet – one single, stunning, bloom held close to your heart.

Bridesmaids do not necessarily have to carry bouquets, either, and the men do not necessarily have to have elaborate buttonholes.

For the girls, why not consider getting them to carry elegant paper fans, or pretty, handmade little beaded or embroidered bags? And the for the lads, how about a flamboyantly coloured pocket handkerchief, or a fabric rosette?

Dried flowers

I'm certainly no expert on things horticultural but friends of mine who are, say that dried flowers really are stunning to look at, and carry the added advantage of being virtually everlasting. Certainly, dried flowers can be purchased from florists and other outlets, but also they can be made to measure, so to speak – provided that there is sufficient time in the run-up to your wedding. And these bouquets and arrangements can be taken home by the bridal party – and guests – to treasure for many years to come. Key "dried flowers" into your favourite search engine.

Fake flowers

Shortly before I started writing this book I read a story in the press about a family in the UK who had decided to create the most eco-friendly wedding they could. One of the many green efforts they made was to create a plethora of fake "flowers" which someone had painstakingly clipped and clamped out of plastic carrier bags.

Now I know that may sound silly, but as far as I can understand the effect was stunning and not only was recycling carried to new heights on that day, but also everyone thought it was an absolutely brilliant idea.

Of course I'm not suggesting that you should frantically collect biodegradable supermarket bags in anticipation of creating your wedding decorations from them. However, there are some alternatives to real or even dried flowers that you can consider.

What about no cut flowers?

Oh, shock, horror! No cut flowers? But let's think about this one. In many "green" weddings in North America, so I'm told, people dump the cut flower ethic altogether in favour of having all wedding decorations courtesy of **potted plants**.

Of course, you could cultivate your own potted flowering plants and use those as decorations. But if this is not a realistic proposition in your case, there are other options. At the time of writing, there are a few companies in the UK offering to rent potted plants out for special occasions. Try keying "potted plants"+hire, or "indoor plants"+hire, into your favourite search engine and see what's on offer. (Tip: do not key in "plant hire" ... if you do you'll get URLs for companies that rent out construction and other heavy equipment!)

The huge advantage of potted plants is, obviously, that they will live to see another day. And it's worth thinking creatively here. Potted plants, as you know, come in all sorts of shapes and sizes. So if you want to go down this route, you can think in terms of large or even very large potted plants (hired of course) to decorate your ceremony and the major areas of your reception, but then add much smaller potted plants — which you buy — as table and other little decorations which guests can take home as wedding favours (see Chapter 9).

One popular option for the larger plants — and one that is readily available here in the UK — is to hire topiary plants. In case you didn't already know, these are usually evergreen trees, plants or shrubs which have been clipped and/or trained into a range of weird, wonderful and often very beautiful shapes. Budget does not permit me to include photographs here, but suffice it to say topiary you can hire can be in the shape of:

- aircraft
- animals
- bells
- bicycles
- birds
- boats
- famous buildings
- fish
- flowers
- lanterns
- urns
- wells
- sporting figures

... plus literally hundreds more shapes and designs.

Some people — wedding organisers — I know filled the church with elegant (hired) topiary plants, one at the end of each pew with others placed strategically around the area. The only other decoration was lots of white ribbon and fairy lights added to some of the topiary. I wasn't at the wedding, but people who were said it looked absolutely stunning.

Other decorations

Flowers and potted plants are by no means the only elements you can use for decorations, especially if your guests know that you're wedding is green-themed. Here is a selection of other items you might like to consider:

- streamers, lanterns, etc. made from recycled paper
- ribbon recycled from secondhand fabrics
- pine cones
- ivy and other vine-type plants, e.g. fresh or dried hops
- foliage and tree branches (fresh)
- pampas grass and other exotic grasses (dried)
- soy-based candles, preferably locally made
- sea shells
- pebbles
- fruit and vegetables (organically grown, locally produced)
- pretty homemade cakes, biscuits and sweets
- fairtrade organic chocolates, and possibly a (fairtrade) chocolate fountain.

This list is just for starters — if you get thinking along these lines I'm sure you'll come up with many more.

Finally, a few words about **balloons** — in a nutshell, they're bad news, especially if they're filled with helium gas and float away. Even if they're aren't helium filled they can get into places where animals and birds will try to eat them and choke to death. In the US they're responsible for killing thousands of sea creatures each year, and several States apparently have banned large scale release of balloons for that reasons. At the time of writing, there are a few companies in the UK advertising biodegradable balloons which is a step in the right direction, but you wonder how long it will take for these balloons to biodegrade — and if they could still be responsible for killing wild creatures in the meantime. For more information key "eco-friendly balloons" into your favourite search engine.

Flowers and decorations

What you can do

- Think hard about using commercial cut flowers as often they are not from fairtade industries and when grown abroad, are brought into the UK by air. Also they may have been affected by numerous different chemicals.

- Locally sourced flowers in season are much greener; organic is even better.

- If you have a long enough lead-time you could grow your own organic flowers for your wedding, or get a green-fingered friend or relative to do it.

- Whatever you do, do not pick wild flowers.

- If you use a florist, check out their approach to environmental issues and avoid using any that can't produce satisfactory answers to your questions.

- See if you can have your flowers and decorations transferred from ceremony to reception, or "double up" with other couples getting married on the same day at the same venue.

- Consider a single, simple bloom instead of a large bridal bouquet, and fabric or paper ornaments for the attendants.

- Consider using dried flowers, either purchased or grown and dried especially for the purpose — they will keep for years.

- Flowers made from paper or fabric (preferably recycled) can look stunning.

- Potted plants can be hired and smaller ones bought and used as gifts for guests.

- Topiary plants are readily available for hire in the UK and can be really attractive.

- Use your imagination to create beautiful decorations from things other than flowers and potted plants.

- Do not use balloons — even biodegradable ones could be harmful to wildlife.

8 Ceremony

There really isn't a great deal to suggest in terms of the eco-friendliness of wedding ceremonies as such, other than in a couple of areas.

Location

The first area to consider is location, which to a large extent we've already looked at in Chapter 3, so I won't go on at length about it here. Just to remind you, though, especially if you are inviting a number of guests you should try to choose a venue that does not require extensive travel for the majority of them. So if you and most of your friends live in the UK, holding your wedding ceremony in an Elvis look-alike chapel in Las Vegas is not an eco-friendly choice. Neither will be a ceremony in a small chapel on a remote Scottish island if most of you live in the south-east, nor will be a civil wedding in the Seychelles if you all live in Manchester.

Content within traditional ceremonies

Obviously if you are having a religious wedding ceremony the content will be dictated to a large extent by the religion concerned. In some religions you can choose music and readings and these can lean towards a green feeling. For example, if you are a Christian you might like to consider the hymn Jerusalem:

Jerusalem
Words: William Blake, c. 1804
Music: Charles Parry

And did those feet in ancient time
Walk upon England's mountain green?
And was the holy Lamb of God
On England's pleasant pastures seen?
And did the countenance divine
Shine forth upon our clouded hills?
And was Jerusalem builded here
Among those dark satanic mills?

Bring me my bow of burning gold!
Bring me my arrows of desire!
Bring me my spear! O clouds, unfold!
Bring me my chariot of fire!
I will not cease from mental fight,
Nor shall my sword sleep in my hand,
Till we have built Jerusalem
In England's green and pleasant land.

To me that has a distinctly environmental feel to it, but of course you may disagree!

Otherwise there is relatively little you can do to secure the eco-friendliness of your religious wedding ceremony other than to ensure that all **documentation** — e.g. Orders of Service — are printed using eco-friendly inks on recycled paper or card, and that **decorations** are as green as possible (see Chapter 7). The other key issue, frivolous though it may seem by comparison, is confetti — see below.

Civil weddings and partnerships

Where you are more at liberty to dictate content is with civil weddings. Although you can't write these ceremonies exactly as you please, you do have some leeway to add extra vows, music and readings to the skeleton of the basic civil procedure. And as these ceremonies are legally accepted, there is no need for you to have an additional ceremony unless you want to, whether that is an actual additional ceremony or a religious blessing.

In addition to the various registry offices in the UK, at the time of writing, there are more than 3,000 other venues licensed to conduct civil weddings and civil partnership ceremonies. At the moment the issue of whether people can get married wherever they want provided the "celebrant" is licensed to perform weddings, is being discussed in high places. Don't hold your breath for results, but with luck this may happen in the future.

Anyway I described most of the currently possible venues in Chapter 3 so once again, I won't bore you with repetition! However, whether you choose to go to an ordinary registry office or to hold your ceremony in one of the approved external venues, here's what you can do to enhance the basics.

Before we get into the "what", though, bear in mind that the main proviso here is that you **run your proposed extra content past the registrar** who will be conducting the ceremony, or at least the person representing the registrar when you make the arrangements. Allow plenty of time, too. There are legal requirements — essentially, at the time of writing, any content you add must be secular in nature, i.e. with no connections with religion whatsoever. You will need to check exactly what requirements are depending on when you read this and in what UK country you are; your local registry office will have the answers.

"Alternative" wedding ceremonies

If you are not religious, or choose to have a non-religious ceremony, there are alternatives.

One such alternative is the "humanist" wedding ceremony. You can find out more about these by keying "humanist weddings" into your favourite search engine, but for now, let's take a look at what these can offer.

Before we go any further please note that I do not support any particular group, company or other organisation offering such weddings – so please, do your own research and make your own decisions here. My job in this book is purely to make suggestions and perhaps open up ideas to you that you might not have thought of yourself.

According to the **British Humanist Association** you can arrange to work with a celebrant and basically hold a ceremony wherever you want, even if it is on a beach or up a tree. Not surprisingly (well, for the UK, anyway), at the time of writing, these ceremonies are not legally acceptable and if you decide to go for this option you will also have to be married by an official registrar if you want the whole thing to be legal.

The advantage of such a ceremony is that, with the celebrant's guidance, you can design it to include pretty much whatever you want, within reason. It's here that you can include whatever secular vows, readings, poems and songs will make the occasion special for you and enhance your environmental beliefs and wishes for the future of the planet.

You might be interested to know that although Humanist celebrants are (currently) not allowed to conduct marriages in England and Wales, celebrants who are simultaneously members of the Humanist Society of Scotland and also authorised to conduct legal marriages, can do both at the same time. Currently, too, Scotland is one of only three countries in the world where Humanist weddings are legally okay; the other two are the USA, and Norway.

For more on this whole issue go: http://www.humanism.co.uk or key "humanist weddings" into your favourite search engine.

Content for civil and alternative ceremonies

On the internet there are ideas a-plenty for environmentally orientated content you can include in your ceremony, if you opt for a civil or alternative ceremony.

For some ideas, try keying the following into your favourite search engine:

- "environmental poetry"
- "environmental music"
- "environmental quotes"

Write your own poems

If you can't find poems or readings that you feel are suitable, you might like to create your own.

Rather than re-invent any wheels, let me reproduce here some information I wrote for another of my weddings books for HowToBooks, *Wedding Speeches For Women*.

If you want to use some poetry forget trying to compete with Wordsworth or Keats; if you want to quote poetry of that type and standard then just help yourself to it. Unless you just so happen to be an accomplished poet yourself, an original poem of your own will be much more effective is it's kept simple and uncomplicated.

Poems these days don't even need to rhyme. However if they're going to work they need to adhere to some sort of rhythm pattern. And if you're a bit of a traditionalist like me you will probably prefer to make the odd few lines, at least, rhyme in that old-fashioned way.

Pick a rhythm for your poem and try to stick to it as closely as possible

Define this to yourself by using the sounds "de DUM de DUM", etc. So the first stanza of a simple poem would be worked out like this:

Some	mot	or	ists	are	ve	ry	kind
de	DUM	de	DUM	de	DUM	de	DUM

To	hors	es	some	what	heat	ed	
de	DUM	de	DUM	de	de	de	

You	slow	and	stop,	with	eng	ines	off,
de	DUM	de	DUM	de	DUM	de	DUM

So	we	can	re	main	seat	ed.	
de	DUM	de	DUM	de	de	de	

This basically gives you the rhythmic structure you need to work from.

Decide which lines should rhyme

In the case of the poem above, it's lines number two and four that rhyme. The way to remember that – and the fact that lines one and three don't rhyme – is: A – B – C – B.

Probably the form I've used here is the easiest, but if you're feeling ambitious you can use pretty well any combination of rhyming scheme you like. Another common form is A – B – A – B, which means that rhymes occur with lines one and three and lines two and four. You could also choose A – A – B – B, etc.

Think of a theme, an idea, a story

As we know, poems are a combination of nice sounding, rhythmic words with a message. It's very easy for the inexperienced poet to get that balance wrong and tend to focus more on the rhythm and rhyme of the words themselves than on what they're actually *saying*.

So think of what you want your poem to say.

Make a list of useful rhyming words

Think of some key words to express your theme or story, then list as many words as you can think of that rhyme with them. Don't forget words that begin with more than one consonant, that are multi-syllabic, etc. Let's say you want to write an amusing short poem about your grandson, the bridegroom, whose name is Will. Here's the list of words you might put down.

Will	love	Gran	groom
bill	above	Nan	boom
fill	dove	man	loom
hill	glove	ban	broom
mill	"guv"	can	room
until	of	fan	bedroom

...and so-on. You may not use all or even any of these, but it helps to give you some guidelines.

Decide how many verses you want and allocate a "task" to each one

In other words, you should try to plan your poem out as far as you can. Bearing in mind that you may be a little restrained by finding words that fit in with the rhythm *and* rhyme with each other, you may want to allow yourself to be a bit flexible here.

So your "poem plan" for this same example might be ...

- Stanza 1:   Will when he was little

- Stanza 2:   Will growing up

- Stanza 3:   Will as a soldier in the Army

- Stanza 4:   Will as a married man

Limericks: an excellent choice for weddings

Limericks are all-time favourites for light-hearted, happy occasions and are surprisingly easy to write. Because of their well-known structure and strong connections with the naughty world of "adult" humour audiences will tend to assume a limerick is going to be funny as soon as you start reading or reciting it.

Also, limericks only have to be vaguely connected with the person or occasion at which they are performed, and in some ways the more out-rageous and/or silly they are the more the audience will appreciate them.

The rhythm of a limerick is always basically the same, although you can add little twiddles to it such as those I have included in brackets:

1. ***De DUM de de DUM de de DUM (de)***
2. ***De DUM de de DUM de de DUM (de)***
3. ***De de DUM de de DUM (de)***
4. ***De de DUM de de DUM (de)***
5. ***De DUM de de DUM de de DUM (de)***

And the rhyming scheme of a limerick is always the same, too; lines one, two and five rhyme with each other, and lines three and four rhyme with each other. So, for the record, the pattern goes A-A-B-B-A.

The trick when writing limericks is to pick line-end words that offer you lots of rhyming options. The other day a friend was going to a birthday party where every guest had to get up and perform a limerick about the birthday boy, a lawyer whose name was a very useful "Tim". This is what I wrote for my friend to say ...

There was a smart lawyer called Tim
Who never quite learned how to swim
But a plaintiff from hell
Threw him into a well
Now Tim's back-stroke's superbly in trim.

I think my job would have been harder if the lawyer's name had been, say, Marcus or Boris!

As with other types of poetry it's a great help if you decide on your theme — which is nearly always expressed in the first line of the limerick — and then list as many words that rhyme with the line-end word of your choice. This gives you a range to choose from for lines one, two and five. In the case of Tim, here, I wrote down the following:

Tim, dim, him, Jim, gym, Kim, limb, rim, vim, whim, slim, swim, trim

I liked the idea of "swim" so it wasn't hard to come up with the idea for lines three and four. And the last line needs a bit of punch, and/or to create a surprise — it's like the punch line of a joke.

Adapting existing poetic material

If you don't want to write your own poem from scratch, you could consider "adapting" some well known material.

This does not necessarily have to be a poem; it can be the words of a song, a hymn, or even a prayer. And any lawyers reading book please calm down. I honestly don't think anyone would ever complain about someone reciting the words to a copyrighted piece at a private event like a wedding. In any case a great deal of popular, well known poems, songs and hymns are either out of copyright or not subject to copyright laws anyway.

Rewritten nursery rhymes

Another type of poem/song you might like to adapt is the nursery rhyme. Here are some examples from two of my joke books, to give you a flavour of how these can work ...

(*Excerpted from Canine Capers, Kenilworth Press 2002*)
Hickory dickory dock
A Collie watched his flock
A bee stung his nose
So hard that he froze
And stood still while his flock ran amok.

(*Excerpted from The Horse Lover's Joke Book, Kenilworth Press 2001*)
Hickory dickory dock
Jump off against the clock
The horse struck one
Four faults were done
"Oh, Hickory dickory ... damn!"

Happy poetry writing!

And a last word about wedding ceremonies

In a word, **confetti**. I know this may seem trivial but it creates a great deal of anxiety in eco-friendly terms because the consequences of throwing it, or its equivalents, can wreak havoc with the environment and wildlife.

As far as I can make out, the throwing of confetti over the bridal couple has its roots in very old, probably pagan marital rituals where the bits of whatever were supposed to represent fertility. That may well be why rice has become a popular option for throwing over the bridal couple as they emerge from the ceremony.

For a number of reasons — not least of which is the reluctance of ceremony venue owners to clean up a sticky mess afterwards — the throwing of confetti in the UK has become rather restricted. Rice, in particular, is a no-no. Despite being a natural substance and in theory biodegradable, dried (as it is) rice hanging around a church yard or other ceremony venue is a pain not only because it clogs up the surrounding areas, but also if birds pick it up and eat it, it is harmful to them. Bird seed may seem a favourable alternative, but it can be dusty and if not picked up in its entirety by birds, it can attract vermin.

Thankfully now many organisations have hopped up on to this bandwagon and are producing **biodegradable confetti** which should satisfy most eco-friendly issues, as well as those raised by ceremony venue owners fed up with having to sweep away the eco-unfriendly variety.

Another popular "green" choice is flower petals. But here you need to ask yourself where those petals come from — are they from local flowers, organically produced, or from airlifted imported flowers raised in non-fairtrade circumstances?

For more information key "biodegradable confetti" into your favourite search engine.

Ceremony

What you can do

● Ensure that the location is as near as possible to where you and the majority of guests live, so transport is kept to a minimum.

● Even if you decide on a religious ceremony, within limits there may be music and readings you can include which are planet-friendly in nature.

● Ensure any documents and other peripherals are created on recycled/recyclable materials.

● With civil weddings, provided you keep your green content secular you may be allowed to include it in your ceremony — check with the registrar.

● You may choose to have an "alternative" wedding ceremony, e.g. a "Humanist" ceremony, which will need to be accompanied by a civil ceremony (except in Scotland).

● Content for poetry, readings, quotes and music can be researched easily on the internet.

● With civil and "alternative" wedding ceremonies you could write your own poems.

● Avoid traditional confetti at all costs, as it can be harmful to wildlife and the environment.

● For issues about photography at and after ceremonies, see Chapter 12.

9 Reception

This is a big one ... from an eco-friendly point of view, a very big one. That's why I have split it into more than one chapter apart from this one — "location" (Chapter 3) "food" (Chapter 10) and "drink" (Chapter 11) as they occupy quite significant spaces in their own right.

As you know, wedding receptions can take many forms other than the traditional ones we have come to accept as the standard choices. Recently some friends of mine who are Viking enthusiasts got married and had an "alternative" wedding ceremony in addition to the civil requirements. The guests were asked to turn up in costume and enjoyed a superb afternoon and evening in what we were assured was true Viking spirit, along with appropriate refreshments which involved a hog roast and numerous other ancient delicacies.

Not all such wedding receptions are eco-friendly, of course, and some may indeed may go against the grain of what we want to achieve in green terms. But my point here, is that you do not need to be restricted to traditional formats of wedding reception unless you particularly want to be. Nowadays almost anything goes.

You'll note that most of my suggestions hinge on food! That's because probably the main element of most wedding receptions is what you give your guests to eat and drink. We'll look at what to serve in Chapter 11, but for now let's consider the various formats you can use and how they rate in eco-friendly terms.

Casual barbecue receptions

Assuming these use acceptable fuels to cook the food, and use organic, locally-grown produce for the barbecue along with organic salads, side dishes, cheeses, breads and desserts, they are relatively green in nature. Guests mingle casually and do not expect gifts, favours, place cards, etc., so cutting down on eco-waste as well as cost.

American-style "pot luck" or guest-participation receptions

This may seem a bit too informal for our rigid British tastes, but think again. The idea here is that instead of wedding gifts, guests bring a dish each to the wedding reception and contribute that to the buffet for all to enjoy. Not only is it an economically bright idea, but also is likely to involve locally grown and certainly locally sourced food, as well as — we hope — the organic variety in addition.

Brunch receptions

These are very popular in North America and are becoming more popular here, with good reason. From a green point of view they are helpful because they are held from late morning to early afternoon, so requiring less in the way of artificial light. From a catering point of view they can encompass pretty well anything you like, from organic range free eggs and locally-cured bacon on locally made organic toasted bread ... to a full lunch menu. The style is less formal than the traditional afternoon/evening reception, and there is usually less alcohol consumption; e.g. organic tea and coffee, fruit juices and perhaps Bucks Fizz made with organic orange juice and organic British fizzy white wine.

Tea receptions

This may seem like a quirky idea but it does cut back on the cost of food and drink and is a lovely variant — especially popular with children. Food wise you serve everything you would at a formal tea party, which in this case can be produced from locally sourced and made sandwiches, cakes, pastries and sweets. Organic tea is the main drink which of course can be supplemented by alcohol if required. The time frame for this type of reception is mid-afternoon until early evening, which is helpful if many guests have distances to travel home and/or have young children who can't really attend an evening reception.

Drinks and canapés

This is an ideal reception format if you want to create a high-luxury, ultra-sophisticated atmosphere without spending a fortune or creating too much eco-damage. The timing will be approximately that of a cocktail party, i.e. early evening, for about two hours. You serve either (organic, possibly even British) champagne, or (organic) cocktails – see Chapter 11 – and a selection of tasty savoury and sweet morsels, some on their own, some on organic mini oat cakes and other locally produced biscuits and crackers. The fact that most guests will remain standing (although of course you should provide seating around the room for those who don't want to stand) means it's very much easier for bride and groom to circulate and talk to everyone. Energy requirements are relatively low, especially if all canapés served are cold, and if the reception is held in the summer half of the year when natural light may be all you need.

Other matters to consider

Let's turn our attention now to some of the other issues surrounding wedding receptions and how we can make them greener.

Lighting

Depending on the venue of your choice, lighting can consume substantial amounts of power which might otherwise be avoided. Consider, as alternatives, at least energy-saving bulbs throughout your reception venue. Beyond that consider, too, the use of soya-based or beeswax-based candles and perhaps more to the point, selecting a time of day for your reception that does not require much, if any, use of artificial light.

Basic items

A horrible term, I know, but one which describes quite efficiently the essential items you need in order to make your reception happen. These include everything from cups to saucers to glasses to knives and forks to plates to napkins to all things beyond. How can these be greener?

Biodegradable everything?

Well, believe it or not, at the time of writing, there are things like biodegradable plates made from sugar cane, and biodegradable cutlery made from potato. Whether you would want to go to that extreme in terms of having them at your wedding reception, I'm not sure. Potentially, the expense of buying these products would far exceed that of hiring good, old fashioned re-usable crockery and cutlery, and would that extra expense be worth it?

Disposable items

Despite being made out of recyclable materials — i.e. paper — disposable plates, cups, glasses, etc. are not necessarily the greenest way forward. Why? Because they are capable of creating a great deal of clutter in recycling and landfill terms. And plastic cutlery not only is unpleasant to use, also it may not be biodegrable/recyclable at all. What eco-experts say now is that conventional crockery and cutlery is best, because it can be re-used again and again and that washing it need not make much of an impression on the eco-filth levels in our drains and sewers, especially if eco-friendly soaps are used.

An even greener outcome...

So what other elements of your wedding reception can we look at in terms of helping towards a greener outcome?

Wedding favours

Probably the most prominent elements are those of decorations, which we looked at in Chapter 7, and also those of wedding favours – or gifts for your guests.

Giving wedding favours, as far as I can make out, is a tradition that comes from North America. However, increasingly it is becoming an issue in the UK for both religious and secular weddings and in any case, giving wedding favours has formed part of many other cultures' traditions for some time.

All it takes is a little imagination, and the wedding favours you choose not only can make a useful contribution to eco-friendliness, but also can be charming, unusual gifts your guests really will treasure. Here are just a few ideas to get you started ...

- bunches of fresh, locally-grown cut herbs tied with organic ribbon
- small herb or other edible plants in tiny pots (little red chilli plants look lovely!)
- small flowering plants in pots (as part of decorations, then guests take home afterwards)
- tree seedlings in small pots
- packs of wildflower or other seeds

- pretty seashells, perhaps with organic sweets inside

- small pieces of locally-made pottery

- small ornaments made from recycled glass

- soya/beeswax candles

- locally-made organic biscuits or sweets

- fairtrade chocolate pralines

- energy-efficient lightbulbs (made glamorous with some foliage decoration!).

Don't forget, however, that there is no unwritten or written rule that says you have to give wedding favours. A greener option is to tell guests (or place a notice in the reception area and on your wedding website) that instead of wedding favours, you're making a donation on behalf of each guest to the charity of your choice.

Entertainment

Entertainment is another area where you can make some green choices. All singing, all dancing live rock bands or DJs/discos with flashing lights and other paraphernalia consume a lot of energy. A lot depends on your musical tastes, of course, but if you happen to like classical, jazz, country, folk or any other genre of predominantly acoustic or semi-acoustic music, using this as your source of entertainment will reduce the power consumption considerably.

If you like country pursuits and your wedding is not in the middle of winter, you could consider holding a **barn dance**. Although the musical elements of these do usually require some electrical amplification — depending on the size of the venue and number of guests — they certainly don't use as much power as a seven piece rock band or even, I suspect a fully-laden DJ set up. And they're great fun! To find organisers in your area, key "barn dances" into your favourite search engine.

A gentler alternative to barn dances is **line dancing**. The music can either be live, again with some amplification needed for large groups, or it can be recorded and played back through a simple sound system. One serious advantage of line dancing is that it's ideal for all age groups, from children right up to elderly folks provided they are reasonably sprightly, so entire family groups can have fun together. Key "line dancing" into your favourite search engine.

Don't forget a **ceilidh** or **Scottish dancing** too — a great energy saver as all you really need is perhaps an accordionist or two and a piper with extremely powerful lungs! A piper will also add gravitas if you use him (I have yet to meet a lady piper, although I'm sure there are some) as punctuation during the earlier part of your reception, such as to announce the meal or herald the cutting of the cake. To find one in your area key ceilidh or "Scottish pipers" into your favourite search engine.

DIY receptions: cleaning up tips

No matter how careful you are to ensure everything is as green as possible when you're planning and conducting your reception, it's quite easy to forget to ensure the cleaning up operation afterwards is as green as possible, too.

If you hold your reception at a specialist venue — i.e. somewhere that does wedding receptions on a package basis — you will have checked out beforehand what their policies are on waste management and recycling, and will be happy with them. If you are organising your reception yourselves, though, you need to be mindful of a number of things.

1. What are you going to do with leftover food? Unless you have a group of hungry friends and family who will take it home and eat it within 24 hours or so, can some be frozen for use later? If not, can you donate it to a local charity like a shelter for the homeless?

2. If you are throwing food, flowers, foliage and other scraps away, have you got appropriate compost heaps and wormeries standing by to take it? Don't forget that meat, oil or dairy products are not suitable for composting or wormeries. Leftover meat and vegetables might be appreciated by a local cat and dog rescue centre, provided the food isn't smothered in rich sauces. Leftover floral or foliage arrangements could go to local seniors' homes.

3. Ensure that all recyclable materials are recycled and don't find their way into the rubbish by mistake. That includes all metal cans and containers, glass bottles, paper, cardboard and plastics.

Reception

What you can do

- Consider styles of reception that do not follow traditional patterns, as often they can be more eco-friendly than the usual types.

- To save on energy usage, see if you can hold your reception in daylight hours and ensure the venue uses either candlelight and/or energy-efficient light bulbs.

- Consider using biodegradable crockery and cutlery if you want to, but don't forget that old-fashioned china and metal are at least reusable and so are reasonably green, too.

- Wedding favours or gifts for guests give you a wonderful chance to make a green statement, and there are some charming options you can choose.

- Instead of wedding favours, make donations to charity on behalf of each guest.

- For musical entertainment, opt for an acoustic or semi-acoustic variety which can be great fun without using masses of power.

- If you're cleaning up after the reception yourselves, be sure you dispose of everything as eco-efficiently as possible.

10 Food

Ever since I started work on this book I have been looking forward to writing this chapter, as I am a confirmed "foodie" — and the more I read about and try out recipes using organic, locally sourced ingredients, the more I am enjoying myself. (And the fatter I'm getting.) Even the most cynical people nearly always have to admit that once you have tried organic fruit, vegetables, meat, poultry, etc., you never want to go back to the non-organic type. And that has little or nothing to do with being eco-friendly, either. It's purely a case that organic, fresh food that hasn't travelled thousands of miles and hasn't been stored in less than ideal circumstances before being driven yet more miles to a supermarket warehouse, *just tastes much better.*

Before we go any further I must make clear that eco-friendly food, in the case of this book anyway, **does not mean purely vegetarian or vegan.** I am aware that in terms of energy and even water, it costs far less to produce a kilo of vegetables than it does a kilo of meat, so from that point of view meat production is not good for the planet. I have read that feedcrop production accounts for more than 30% of all arable land on our planet; I have read that around 30% of our land surface which previously was habitat for wildlife is now given over to livestock; I have read that grazing land occupies more than 25% of all our land that isn't frozen over; I've also read widely about methane, carbon dioxide and ammonia emissions from livestock as well as it being responsible for more than 50% of our sediment and erosion problems. I know, I know.

However — and this is a big "however" — when it comes to your wedding reception, as I've suggested earlier in this book we need to keep a balance between what is eco-correct and what is taking the whole thing to extremes. In ordinary circumstances it's likely that at least some of your guests will be meat eaters. And provided that meat, poultry, and also fish/seafood are organic, locally produced where appropriate and come from sustainable sources, they are green enough to go into this book. Needless to say, I have included many vegetarian and vegan options too, so you can make your choices as you wish. But to exclude meat altogether would, in my not-so-humble opinion, be inappropriate here. Within reason, I believe you can eat meat and still be green.

Local is greenest

One of the key elements of being green is eco-consumerism, which as you know essentially means supporting local businesses and especially meat and poultry producers, in the light of increasing price squeezing from supermarkets selling ridiculously cheap imported products. The fact that many of these taste of nothing and shrink to half their artificially plumped-up on-shelf size when you cook them, still doesn't stop people buying such rubbish in droves at the expense of local organic farmers who care well for their animals, avoid all unnatural chemicals and try to sustain the local economy for the benefit of their communities.

This element of eco-consumerism has even acquired its own name in the USA; the word is *locavore* … meaning someone who eats only local produce! When you think that in North America the average distance travelled by food from producer to your dinner table is around 1,500 miles, you can understand why they are even more concerned than we are here in the UK about reducing "food miles".

Locavores also are concerned about knowing the origins of our food, where it is farmed, where and how it is sold, etc. That's hard to do if it has been flown in from Argentina or Thailand. At the time of writing, the locavores have a fledgling movement under way on the west coast of the US, encouraging people to eat only food produced within around a 100 mile radius of where they live, which is not much of a distance in North American terms. Failing that, they prioritise food that is organic, and failing that food produced by a family farm or other local business. To learn more of the locavores go to: http://www.locavores.com. (I hope by the time you read this they are still active – I think it's a great idea.)

There are other reasons why locally sourced organic – and even non-organic – food can be better for us and for the planet, too.

With food that has travelled many hundreds or thousands of miles, inevitably it will have been handled by a large number of systems and groups and teams and distribution centres and logistics warehouses and transport companies and who knows what else. With each additional exposure, that food becomes more vulnerable to infection or pollution.

And as you know with the massive industries our food production have become, we have seen increasing problems with infectious diseases like vCJD, BSE in cattle, salmonella in eggs and poultry, plus other livestock diseases like foot-and-mouth, bird flu and blue tongue. Just where the responsibility for these problems lies is not within my remit to comment on. However, I don't know about you, but all these issues encourage me to seek food sources — and not just meat and poultry — from local suppliers whom I know to be honest, clean, caring, humane and decent, whether entirely organic or not. I know that even they are not immune to the terrible mass diseases (e.g. bird flu can be and often is spread by wild birds) but all the same, industrialisation and mass-production of food by us humans has a great deal to answer for.

Farmers' markets and shops

This is an interesting food source, and its definition varies from area to area and from country to country. As with so many other things, you need to **adopt a "buyer beware" approach** with organic food and particularly that which supposedly is produced locally. Check it out, ask questions, and don't be afraid to challenge what you see and what you're told.

When I am in Canada (where I come from originally) going to a farmer's market means pulling up just off the road in the spring, summer and early autumn months to some stalls where the farmer on whose land this is, and his friends and family, are selling the vegetables, fruit and other things they generate on the premises. You don't get fresher than that and the produce is truly delicious.

Here in the UK there are some enterprises like that but in my experience, so far at least, they tend not to be so energetic.

Farmers' markets over here often can be no more than an excuse for businesses to sell their wares on an outdoor platform under the guise of being organic and planet-friendly. My feelings towards those are mixed — especially as the last time I went to my local farmer's market the first stall I saw was selling delicatessen-type delicacies and the first display to catch my eye was labelled "Moroccan olives". Oh, yes — very local to mid-Bedfordshire, England.

With all due respects to those markets, however, there are also many local or at least regional traders who sell their produce — like delicious goat's cheese, goat sausages, organic range-free poultry and innumerable other things — which do deserve an organic, locally-produced label.

One thing that does help to regiment farmers' markets in the UK is their trade body, the National Association of Farmers' Markets, whose website you can view at: http://www.farmersmarkets.net.

There are various other food initiatives in place in the UK to enhance our access to good, pure, locally-produced organic food. And although these may not necessarily be of much help in sourcing food for your wedding reception, you might like to know about them all the same. Have a look in Chapter 15 for some more contact URLs.

Farm shops are another genre of business that can trade on the organic/eco-friendly ticket without necessarily deserving to.

One farm shop I go to regularly sells such items as avocados, lemons, oranges, limes, tomatoes out of season and other fruits which I just know have not been grown in sunny Bedfordshire. The justification for buying such fruits? Well, without doubt they have been imported, but at least any profit obtained by the business through selling them goes towards maintaining a local business, so that's a contribution towards eco-consumerism. And that same farm shop does sell a large number of locally produced items, too.

Should you buy ingredients for your wedding feast from farm shops? Okay, they may include imported products to help ramp up their sales and profits, but at least they are local businesses whose stock consists largely of local produce. Once again, a balanced view is called for, and overall, they probably are good news.

Ethical, but not local

A number of food types are extremely popular, but are not cultivated in the UK — largely because our climate is unsuitable. This includes citrus fruits, avocados, some species of pears and apples, mangoes, grapes, bananas, etc. Whether we like it or not this produce has to be imported into the UK at least from southern Europe and often from further afield.

To offset this, there are a number of **fairtrade** and other, similar "sustainable" initiatives in place to ensure that at least the people and businesses producing these goods are treated fairly and in some instances are helped significantly to improve their quality of life. For example, currently one of the large UK supermarket chains has a programme in place in South Africa whereby they fund projects at a number of farms to help with adult training, housing, medical issues, crèches and so-on.

You may want to check out such initiatives when you source these items; they may not be organic and certainly are not locally produced, but in buying them you are helping to achieve some good for the planet all the same.

Beware the scams and conflicts

Although most food manufacturers, caterers and other food-related businesses are honest — plus the fact that ingredient and content claims on food labelling are quite strictly policed here in the UK — there are still a few that slip through the net for one reason or another. Some foods that are labelled "natural", for example, only have to contain a small percentage of natural ingredients to qualify.

Foods labelled as "organic" may well be so, but may have travelled thousands of miles by air or ship (shipping causes pollution too — see Chapter 14) and may not even come from a fairtrade source. Food labelled as "fairtrade" may not be organic. And so it goes on.

As always you need to make considered decisions about the food to serve at your wedding reception based — yes — on green criteria, but also based on common sense and more pressing, realistic priorities like availability, whether locally sourced or not, and whether genuinely wholesome and tasty.

Yes, organic can cost more

It may seem unfair but for the time being at least, it's an economic reality. Food and drinks that come from far-away countries where labour is cheap and no-one is too fussy about chemicals, hygiene or any other potentially costly niggle, probably is going to be cheaper to buy than good, clean food that is grown with UK or at least European legal systems and tax laws, distributed — even locally — by vehicles paying more than £1 per litre of fuel at the time of writing and rising. However, here we risk straying into the area of politics which certainly is a bad idea.

To help offset the extra cost of using local, organic produce, you may want to consider lower-cost reception options like barbecues, brunches, teas, and drinks/canapés, as I outlined in Chapter 9.

Catering – your choices

Unless you are a professional or very keen amateur cook and have plenty of time in hand immediately before your wedding, it makes sense **not to attempt to create the food yourself**. Leaving it in the capable hands of a good friend or relative can be a wonderful solution, provided that you can count on that person being capable of delivering what you need, on time.

If there is any doubt on those counts, though, you are far better off hiring a **professional caterer**. If you key "organic caterers" into your favourite search engine you will find a reasonable selection but at the time of writing there aren't that many established in the UK, and those that are already trading tend to be located near the main conurbations.

However, there is no reason why any caterer can't produce a wonderful organic spread made from local produce, provided that you work together to ensure the menu and ingredients all come from appropriate places.

So, let's now look at some organic/locally produced options and how you can use them.

Okay, so what's in season when?

We are very lucky here in the UK because we have — at least — vegetables and meat, poultry, game and so-on which provide us with a year-round menu availability of one sort or another.

Obviously, the late spring, summer and early autumn months give us a lot more leeway in terms of food choice, but a winter wedding is not necessarily doomed to the doldrums should you want to enjoy organic, locally produced seasonal dishes at those times.

My list of seasonal foods is by no means complete — there are many more. However, what I have included should give you a good basis on which to start building your menus.

Winter-spring months

Let's start with the (supposedly) dire winter/early spring months of **January to March**. What's in season then?

Carrots

Did you know that carrots originally came from Asia and were used as medicine? And, that carrots are closely related to parsley? They're chock full of Vitamin A and beta carotene plus other vitamins and minerals, plus they're grown almost year round here in the UK. In terms of wedding reception food they are very useful as side vegetables to a main dish, as hot vegetables combined with, say, chopped shallot and butter plus a little sugar, honey and/or a squirt of lemon as a buffet dish, and of course raw, grated as a salad ingredient either alone or combined with other vegetables like celeriac, cabbage, lettuce, etc.

Pears

These can be used not only in a number of dessert dishes, but also as an accompaniment to main dishes involving pork, chicken, guinea fowl, etc.

Scallops

I'm allergic to shellfish so I don't touch it even with a barge pole, and unless you're certain no-one amongst your wedding guests has a shell-fish allergy, I would avoid this one. However, if you are certain there is no problem, you can rest assured that scallops can (a) be sourced in relatively local terms − e.g. Scotland − and (b) are sustainable, especially as they are now farmed extensively in Scotland and elsewhere in the UK, as far as I can understand.

Turnips

Turnips aren't very glamorous as vegetables but if they are small, they are incredibly tasty as side vegetables.

Other vegetables

Those likely to be in season consist of **squash**, **cabbage**, **leeks**, **parsnips**, **celeriac**, and **shallots**. Later in the season you'll also get **chicory**, plus some early **radishes** (delicious in salads) and even early **parsley** which you can use as a garnish for so many savoury dishes, as well as in salads. Finally, you might be able to choose from **purple sprouting broccoli**, **sorrel**, **beetroot** and of course the ever-galloping **mint**.

Leeks

Leeks come on stream later in this period − they are incredibly useful vegetables not only in their own right, but as accompaniments to a wide variety of casseroles and other main dishes.

Fruits?

Not many, but there might just be some forced **rhubarb** around — so tasty in a crumble.

Other foods

Now, how about **flesh**-based foods in the winter-spring period?

Obviously there are all the main **meat and poultry** options, and nowadays it's possible to get fresh, locally produced meat and poultry all year round. In season will be certain types of **game**, if you're willing to eat that, plus **goose** — and if you're into shellfish, **lobster**.

Also as winter moves towards spring you might like to look at **guinea fowl**, plus for the sea-based taste, **halibut** (sustainable) and **mussels**.

Spring months

Now, let's move on to the **spring months** of April, May and June.

Spring lamb

For meat eaters, spring lamb is coming into season now and unless you are a confirmed veggie, to my mind there is nothing more delicious than fresh organic lamb cooked in a number of different ways. Although lamb is available later in the year in the UK, that which you can get in the spring really does have the edge in taste.

Rosemary

To go with your lamb (amongst many other things) rosemary is at its peak now too. Not only can you use the leaves and stems to flavour anything from roast lamb to barbecues, but also you can use the flowers as salad ingredients and even as additions to some sweet dishes like fruit salad or sorbet.

Salmon trout

Still in the flesh (well, fish) department we have the availability now of salmon trout (also called sea trout) which can make a tasty starter dish for a sit-down reception meal. Later on — from June onwards for a few weeks — you can also consider **grey mullet**, provided that it comes from a good, sustainable UK source.

Crab

Also, crab becomes a seasonal option, particularly from our east coast ... having spent a week in Cromer, Norfolk, years ago despite being allergic to shellfish, I can vouch for that one! However if you are not allergic and want to include this shellfish in your reception menu, now — probably — is the time to do it, although proponents of Cromer crab production say that it's available from spring to mid-winter.

Duck

Then, if you like duck, this is the time to consider it. Although farmed duck is available all year round in the UK, this period is when it will be at its best.

Greens

Early **spinach** becomes available now, and although not everyone's favourite as a cooked vegetable, its leaves are delicious in salads which can be useful for buffet-style wedding receptions. Other vegetables coming into season now include **watercress, radishes, kale** — increasingly popular for its health-giving properties — as well as **carrots**, of course, plus **spring onions**, and certain types of **mushrooms**. If you like the taste of the sea, **samphire** becomes available now and is particularly tasty served with fish.

And as for **asparagus**, well – should your wedding fall within the period between the end of April and the middle of June or thereabouts, UK-grown specimens will make a truly delicious contribution to your buffet, sit-down meal or even canapé-based reception. A bit later on you'll find that **broad beans** become available and these can make some excellent contributions to salads for a buffet meal, as well as being vegetable choices to accompany meat, or as part of vegetarian delicacies.

Also towards the end of June you'll find that UK-grown **courgettes** start to become available in their "baby marrow" formats ... although some growers like to hang on to them until they become enormous marrows!

Needless to say UK-grown **lettuce** starts to come into its own now, which certainly makes salad creation easier. Some varieties of **peppers** mature now too, as well as (previously mentioned) spring onion, plus chive, parsley, cress, and several other plants which will contribute to an incredibly tasty green salad.

Fruits

Towards the end of this period you may start to see early varieties of British **strawberries**. Not only can you enjoy the cultivated kind, but also so-called **wild or Alpine strawberries** (they're growing wild in my garden, anyway) which have a slightly smokey, aromatic flavour and are superb served with ice cream or sorbet, or even as an accompaniment to some meat or roast vegetable dishes. At the same time early varieties of **gooseberry** become available which can be made into delicious dessert dishes as well as making contributions to salads of several kinds. And should you be

Scottish-inclined, you might even find that there are some early-maturing **tayberries** in the offing ... interesting berries which taste somewhere between a raspberry and a blackberry. They can add some oomph to early summer fruit salads as well as some more "off the wall" savoury dishes.

Summer months

In the UK this is the time when locally produced foods — particularly fruit and vegetables — are at their finest and most prolific. Pretty much everything you will find at local stores or farm shops will be locally pro-duced at this time — or at least should be — and for your wedding reception menus you will have a huge choice of options.

Aubergines are hardly indigenous to the UK, at least not originally, but having been introduced to Britain about three centuries ago they now grow abundantly and prolifically in our climate. Along with other highly roastable vegetables like **courgettes, fennel, peppers,** etc. they make delicious vegetarian hot dishes as well as being useful as side accompa-niments to main courses.

Tomatoes, of course, are in full flow now in the UK and as you know they can contribute towards anything from salads to sauces to casseroles ... in fact almost to anything. **Peas** are also in season at this time and represent a popular side dish. Don't forget, too, that **watercress** is still around and is delicious not only in salads but as a side accompaniment to numerous meat and vegetarian main courses. UK-grown **sweetcorn** becomes available towards the end of this period and UK-grown **lettuce** is in abundance now too.

On the fruits side you're still seeing **strawberries**, of course, along with many other summer fruits like raspberries and their similar cousins. You might also be seeing some early **apple** and **pear** varieties.

Autumn months

Once again, this period provides with a cornucopia of choices.

In season and in abundance: **mushrooms, kale, pumpkin, marrow, beet-root, courgettes, plus a few!** All give you the potential for some lovely side dishes (should you be including meat) or for incorporating into main dishes within the vegetarian/vegan remit.

Fruits include **plums, apples, damsons,** and many others as well, of course, as **elderberries** and **blackberries**. There is a wide choice for delicious desserts and also as ingredients to go into meat dishes.

Lamb is a popular choice now too, although at this time of year it tends to be more strongly flavoured than what is produced in the spring. That's because by this time the meat is more mature. Roasted, or slow-braised with onions, garlic, rosemary and other autumn vegetables, it is a superb choice for a main course at a sit-down meal.

If you don't have an eco-problem with **game** – e.g. sustainable, farmed **partridge, pheasant, duck, venison,** etc. – this is the time of year when you can enjoy it at its best. I know; I dislike the thought of killing these attractive creatures for sporting purposes, but when it is for food and they are bred for that purpose, it should not be thrown out of the "green" portfolio.

On the fishy side, **oysters** are now in season – in fact they are in season in any month that has the letter "R" in it. These are found in a variety of relatively local areas including the coast of Kent. If you're sure that your guests are not allergic to shellfish by all means include these as a starter to a sit-down meal. However, if you are unsure, you can still include them as part of a canapé or buffet reception; just make sure they are well identified.

And from November to December?

This, according to many sources, in the UK is a gastronomic no-man's-land. Actually, it couldn't be further from the truth. Blessed as we are in the UK with a mild winter climate this is a time when all kinds of delicious goodies emerge, fresh from our own fields and pastures.

Of the many vegetables now available you can take your pick from **Brussels sprouts** which begin to mature now, as well as **leeks, swede, potatoes, red and white cabbage, white celery, celeriac, beetroot, turnips, parsnips** and of course, **chestnuts**. Despite not being as plentiful as in the summer season, fruits are still available including **apples** and **pears**, plus lovely mature **pumpkin** (so much more taste than the earlier specimens harvested in October for Halloween) and **quinces** (sharp, smoky and delicious in a home made jelly).

Organic, range-free **goose**, **turkey** and **duck** is widely available now in the run-up to the holiday season, provided you're not threatened with an epidemic of avian influenza as we are at the time of writing. Turkey, in particular, is a popular choice as a main dish for large groups at a sit-down meal, but if your wedding reception is at this time of the year your guests already may well be eating turkey as part of their holiday season celebrations and so you might like to choose something different for your wedding!

Your wedding cake

Traditionally in the UK, wedding cakes tend to be of the old-fashioned "fruit" cake. Whereas this type offers a number of advantages — not least of which is the fact that it can be made well in advance of the wedding, and lasts for some time afterwards — many of its ingredients, although they can be organic, have to come from outside of the UK. This normally would include the currants, sultanas, raisins, mixed peel, glazed cherries, brown sugar, brandy, plus spices and lemon rind.

There are many appetising **alternatives to the traditional fruit cake.**

Plain or flavoured sponge cakes are a good alternative and can be made almost entirely from UK-sourced, organic ingredients. To flavour these you may need to resort to fairtrade chocolate, bananas and other imported fruits. Alternatively, you could go for carrot cake – one of my favourites and one which can, once again, be made almost entirely of UK sourced organic ingredients – including the carrots.

There are many recipes accessible via the internet which are made from entirely vegetarian or vegan ingredients, too – including carrot cake!

To start your search for an appropriate wedding cake recipe, or supplier, key one or more of the following search terms into your favourite search engine:

- "vegetarian wedding cakes"
- "vegan wedding cakes"
- "diabetic wedding cakes"
- "organic wedding cakes".

Some sample wedding menus

I have been very lucky to obtain the participation of **Daphne Lambert**, award-winning chef, nutritionist, author and teacher who offers "green" cooking courses based at her beautiful premises in Herefordshire, which is also the site of a lovely hotel and restaurant. (See her website at:

http://greencuisine.penrhos.com) Daphne has put together some sample menus for a variety of different wedding reception types, in different seasons, to give you some ideas of how you can create a truly glorious organic (though not all locally sourced) wedding feast ...

Sit-down full meals

Summer lunch or dinner

Courgette soup with chive blossoms
Grilled fillet of brill with marsh samphire
Elderflower and gooseberry fool with elderflower shortbread

Winter lunch or dinner

Fennel and almond soup
Lemon, honey and thyme chicken with roast vegetables
Apple tarte tatin with cinnamon ice-cream

Spring lunch or dinner

Spring salad of garden leaves and quails eggs
Chicken braised in red wine, or ginger and lime marinaded hake
Rhubarb crumble with orange ice-cream, or chocolate terrine

Buffet spreads

Summer buffet #1

Tomato and rocket salad with goat's cheese
Fresh baked bread
Honey and thyme roast chicken
Salmon fish cakes

Red peppers with quinoa stuffing
Roast vegetables with cous cous
Summer salad leaves with herb dressing
New potato salad
Cucumber salad with coriander and yogurt
Alfalfa, carrot and beetroot salad
Raspberries with hazlenut meringue
Chocolate mousse cake
Vanilla ice-cream with peaches in brandy syrup

Summer buffet # 2

Melon with raspberry sorbet
Fresh baked bread
Chicken satay with cashew nut sambal
Grilled fillets of salmon, sea bass and red mullet with herb salsa
King prawns with smoked pepper dip
Roast vegetables with lemon and mint couscous
Tomato and mozzarella salad
White beans and flageolets with summer beans, lemon and tarragon
Garden lettuces and rocket with hazelnut and shallot dressing
Blackcurrant rippled ice-cream
Strawberries with rose syrup and crème fraiche
Peach and almond tart

Vegetarian buffet

Roast pepper and tomato soup with basil
Fresh baked bread
Vegetable lasagna
Roast summer vegetables with tabbouleh
Millet and tofu cakes with harissa
Falafel with hummus and a cucumber and mint salad

Potato salad with chives
Grilled halloumi with summer beans
Salad leaves with tarragon-lemon dressing
Coconut ice with chocolate sauce
Strawberry pavlova
Raspberry cheesecake

Autumn buffet

Carrot soup with ginger
Fresh baked bread
Roast pesto chicken
Butternut squash lasagne
Salmon 'en-croute'
Roast vegetables with croutons
Cucumber, tomato, goat's cheese and mint salad
Green salad with herb dressing
Potato gratin
White chocolate ice-cream with hot blackberry sauce
Apple tart with cream

Winter buffet

Carrot soup with ginger
Fresh baked bread
Honey roast chicken
Butternut squash lasagne
Salmon 'en-croute'
Potato, leek and fennel gratin
Broccoli salad with tahini dressing and roast pine kernels
Winter salad leaves with orange-thyme dressing
White chocolate ice-cream with hot blackberry sauce
Apple tart with cream

Summer fork buffet

Salmon fishcakes
Penne with roasted vegetables and toasted pine kernels
Chicken satay with spicy peanut dip
Little gem, alfalfa and tomato salad with basil
Foccacia
Local cheeses with oatcakes
Lemon tart
Chocolate and raspberry roulade

Finger buffet

Cruditées
Honey and thyme glazed vegetable brochettes
Roast vegetable crostinis with cashew nut pesto
Home cured, herb marinaded salmon with horseradish crème fraiche
Thai-spiced chicken with a lime and coriander dressing

Canapé ideas

Parmesan biscuits
Carpaccio of beef
Roast vegetable bruschetta
Wild mushroom and shallot tartlet
Smoked salmon crostini
Baby dulse scones with smoked salmon
Baby sun-dried tomato scones with baba ganoush
Baby horseradish scones with British roast beef
Chocolate brownie
Apple beignet

Sadly, I haven't room here to include Daphne's recipes, but if there is one dish that really takes your fancy she might share it with you if you ask her nicely! You can get in touch with Daphne via her website, at: http://greencuisine.penrhos.com.

Food

What you can do

- Meat and poultry are not very green, but within reason they are acceptable as part of your wedding menu.

- If you need to prioritise between local and organic, local might be greener.

- Don't be hoodwinked into thinking farmers' markets and farm shops sell only local produce.

- If in doubt, check out: http://www.farmersmarkets.net.

- Watch for labels saying food is "natural" — it may only be a little bit natural!

- Know the difference between fairtrade and organic and make your decisions based on common sense.

- Check terms and other related issues on: http://www.soilassociation.org.

- Be prepared to pay more for organic food.

- Don't attempt to cater your wedding yourself unless you really know how to handle it.

- Choose your menu according to foods that are in season around your wedding date.

- Traditional fruit cake is not the best choice if you want to go organic/locally sourced.

- Other types of cake can be wholly organic using only locally sourced ingredients.

- Start your creative menu planning with the ideas from Daphne Lambert.

11 Drinks

There is quite a major move going on, at the time of writing, towards more planet-friendly drinks, and in particular alcoholic drinks.

Many supermarkets now are promoting **fairtrade** wines, and **organic** and **biodynamic** wines are becoming more popular. The British wine industry — i.e. locally-sourced wine — is not exactly large, and currently only a few British vineyards are producing organic products.

Organic beers are appearing in Britain now, but growing conditions are such that the organic hops from which the beer is made currently are having to be imported. Organic cider isn't such a problem, and this is a growing market in the UK.

It's also possible to buy the following drinks in organic form:

- cordials
- juices
- squashes
- ginger beer
- lemonade (fizzy)
- grappa and similar strong distillations
- various liqueurs, especially calvados
- cognac
- other brandies
- vodka
- gin
- whisky
- rum (white and golden)
- sherry

- muscat

- port

...etc.

However, not all of these, by any means, are produced in the UK.

Choose your own balance

As always, you need to balance your desire to use planet-friendly products for your wedding, in line with other considerations such as cost and convenience. To help you, here is how the main types of "eco-friendliness" relate to both alcoholic and non-alcoholic drinks.

Organic

This term can apply to all types of wine, beer, cider, spirits, liqueurs, soft drinks, tea and coffee. It means that the drink has been made according to organic guidelines, i.e. without or with minimal use of chemicals like pesticides, etc. Organic products are not necessarily produced locally so are apt to involve food miles — in some cases, thousands of food miles. Also, organic drinks are not necessarily fairtrade.

When you consider the chemicals that are used in conventional winemaking today, you can understand why organic methods are being encouraged. According to Friends Of The Earth there are traces of something like 240 chemicals in most ordinary wine, the result of spray residues, and it takes about one tonne of chemicals to produce just 8,000 bottles of burgundy. Not only is this alarming where the wine itself is concerned, but also there is a nasty backlash to the soil in the area of the vineyards. Friends Of The Earth claim that due to chemical pollution some of this soil in the classic French wine producing areas now contains less microbial life than does the sand in the Sahara desert.

And if you want another upside to organic wine, think of this ... because the use of sulphites is kept right down in production, organic wine has far lower levels of sulphur than ordinary wine. With sulphur being thought to be the main culprit in hangovers, what this means is that by drinking organic wine you should suffer far less from "the morning after" syndrome. That's something you may well appreciate on your wedding day ... and the next morning!

Sustainable

A number of countries are running sustainable wine making projects and these essentially form an umbrella structure in which producers are encouraged to use natural/organic/biodynamic growing and production methods. I assume that the "sustainable" element here probably connects with the way that organic/biodynamic methods are far less harmful to the soil and surroundings.

Biodynamic wine

This is an interesting concept and in fact was around long before the whole "organic" movement got going. It has been described as not so much a way of farming as a way of thinking. It's organics-plus, really; organic methods enhanced by such things are herbal and homeopathic additions, special composts and other bespoke natural preparations, combined with observation of and harmonisation with the sun and moon, with the entire, overall farming activity performing in an holistic manner.

Biodynamics were originated back in the 1920s by the Austrian scientist Rudolf Steiner who sought to combine the benefits of the material and spiritual worlds in a number of ways, including agriculture. Today, bio-dynamic farmers have varying views of Steiner's teachings, and a variety of specific biodynamics methods have sprung up in different places. Partly because the concept has previously been seen as a bit "alterna-tive" it has only become widely known in the late twentieth and early twenty-first centuries.

As for the taste and desirability of biodynamic wine? It's called "watch this space", and make your own decisions.

British drinks

This has the advantage of offering locally grown and produced drinks, so cutting right back on the food miles.

Although they may or may not make organic **beer**, there are a number of small breweries making beer and/or "real" ale for their local commu-nities and you may wish to choose the nearest one to your wedding reception as a supplier, if you're going to serve beer.

A great deal of **cider** — both organic and non-organic — is produced in the UK, so you shouldn't have too much trouble finding some if you wish to serve it, or include it as part of a punch.

Some organic **spirits** and **liqueurs** are made in the UK, and these can provide a welcome boost to cocktails and punches.

Non-alcoholic juices, cordial and squashes can be found quite widely in farm shops and other locally-focused retail outlets, and many of these will be organic, too. To keep these as "green" as possible you may want to choose such drinks made only from fruit grown in the UK, like apples, pears, strawberries, raspberries, blackberries, elderflowers, elderberries, etc. Sparkling varieties of some of these drinks are usually available, too.

And finally, **British wine**. Although there are only a few British vineyards producing organic wine, at the time of writing, this number is likely to increase, and even if the wine producers are not organic they do tend to stick to as natural and traditional methods of growing and making as possible.

Vines for wine making apparently were first introduced into Britain by the Romans, and during the Middle Ages became very popular. However for one reason and another — possibly linked to our comparatively inappropriate climate — the vineyards declined over the following centuries before finally enjoying something of a renaissance in the second half of the twentieth century.

Currently there are less than 400 registered vineyards in the UK which in 2006 produced well over 3 million bottles, the majority of which were of the white variety. It's interesting to note that home-produced wine in the UK accounts for just one percent of total UK wine consumption, which means we get through rather a lot of bottles … as they say, "do the math!"

However there are now some very tasty English wines including fizzy varieties of dry white which (a) are a very acceptable alternative to champagne or its foreign clones and (b) are not expensive, so making them very useful for wedding receptions.

As I say, not all — in fact few — of these British wines are likely to be organic, although in time I imagine more and more wine producers in this country will move in that direction. However, from the point of view of a green balance, you may feel it's better to use non-organic British wine for your reception than to serve organic wine that has travelled thousands of miles to get here. Don't forget that investing in your local or regional economy can be worth a great deal in "green" terms, too.

In making your choice for punches, cocktails etc., remember that a great many delicious fortified wines are made in the UK from a variety of home-grown fruits, as well as mead, which is made from honey.

Other considerations

Corks or screw caps?

When buying wine these days we have been led to believe that screw caps are better for us and for the environment as they don't require us to chop down cork-producing trees. However, it seems this could be something of a marketing-led re-arrangement of the truth. To begin with, stripping the bark off cork trees does not require them to be cut down; the bark regrows, and nine years later can be stripped again. Some cork trees can live for as long as 500 years.

Most of the world's cork is produced in the forests of Spain and Portugal and these forests are known to be among the top 10 biodiversity locations in the world. Should demand for cork drop dramatically, economics would dictate that many of these forests should be destroyed and replaced by other, more financially viable agriculture or even development that is nowhere nearly as planet-friendly. Retaining the cork industry means retaining innumerable species of wildlife, not to mention the thousands of traditional cork farming families' livelihoods. And cork is ideal for recycling or composting, as it decomposes without giving off any toxins.

Serving imported wine anyway?

It seems that to ship just three bottles of Chardonnay over here from Australia results in the emission of well over 800 grams of CO2. If you want to offset that, you can do so by planting a tree, which will take care of about 250 bottles' worth of CO2 — probably enough to cover your wedding reception plus some. But check Michael Bloch's article in Chapter 14 before you invest there.

Where to find these drinks

All the organic and other eco-friendly drinks I have suggested in this chapter are available via the internet — simply key the appropriate term into your favourite search engine. In addition, you should be able to find a reasonable amount of the products in supermarkets, health food shops, farm shops and even wine merchants and off-licences.

Some alcoholic drink ideas

Rather than suggest exact measure, I am stating the proportions of the ingredients so you can adjust the quantities according to the number of people you're serving. Garnishes can be almost anything you like, e.g. slices of fruit, sprigs of herbs like mint or borage, edible organic flowers, organic fresh cherries, etc. Bear in mind that I have adapted these recipes from ordinary ones which I have found on a variety of websites and in books, but I have not had the opportunity to try them all out myself. (If I did I would probably become an alcoholic!) So if you fancy using any of them do try them out on a small scale yourself first, and be sure you like them. It's your wedding, after all!

Organic White Rum Cocktail

2 parts organic white rum
1 part fairtrade lime juice
1/6 part organic grenadine
Shake ingredients together with some ice, and pour into cocktail glasses.

Green Black Velvet

Equal parts draught Guinness and dry, fizzy British white wine (organic if possible)
Combine in champagne glasses.

Fairtrade Buck's Fizz

Fairtrade freshly-squeezed orange juice
Dry, fizzy British white wine (organic if possible)
Combine together in champagne glasses, in whatever proportions you prefer!
If you want to add a little kick to this recipe you can include a dash of an orange-based (preferably organic) liqueur.

Eco-Friendly Tom Collins

$2\frac{1}{2}$ parts organic gin
1 part fresh fairtrade lemon juice
1/6 part white sugar dissolved in a little water
Fizzy natural British spring water
Place first three ingredients in glass or jug and top up with the fizzy water.

Eco Daiquiri

$2\frac{1}{2}$ parts organic white rum
1 part fresh fairtrade lime juice

1/6 part white sugar dissolved in a little water
Shake all ingredients together with some ice, and strain into appropriate glasses.

Eco Frozen Daiquiri Deluxe

As above, but put all ingredients in a blender along with the ice and add some soft fruit like fairtrade banana or locally-sourced organic berries. Yum ... my favourite.

Green-aholic Coffee

1/3 part fairtrade brown sugar
2 1/2 parts organic whisky or brandy
5 parts hot fairtrade and/or organic coffee
1 part whipped locally produced organic cream
Place sugar and whisky in heatproof cup or mug and mix well, then add coffee and mix again. Finally add the whipped cream very carefully, pouring it over a large spoon so it remains at the top.

Recycling Russian Cocktail

5 parts organic vodka
1 part fresh fairtrade lime juice
Organic ginger beer
Place lime juice and vodka into a container with some ice, and fill up with the ginger beer.

Eco-Conscious Pimms

Readymade Pimms, or "fake" Pimms as follows:
1 part organic port or sweet sherry
2 parts red vermouth

3 parts organic gin

$\frac{1}{4}$ part organic orange-based liqueur

Sliced fairtrade citrus fruits as available

Sliced locally-grown organic apples, pears, strawberries

Thin slices of locally-grown organic cucumber

Sprigs of fresh, locally-grown organic mint, borage, basil

Plenty of ice, especially on a warm summer's day

Mix all the above together in a large container and fill up with either organic fizzy lemonade, or organic ginger ale.

Bio-Friendly Mary

1 part organic vodka

4–6 parts (to taste) freshly-made juice from locally-grown organic tomatoes

1/8 part organic Worcestershire sauce (or to taste)

Combine the ingredients and serve on ice with a slice of fresh fairtrade lemon.

Ethical Piña Colada

1 part organic white rum

2 parts fresh fairtrade pineapple juice

1 part fairtrade coconut cream

Ice

Whizz all ingredients in a blender, and pour into individual glasses.

Sustainable Sangria

8 parts organic brandy

48 parts organic or biodynamic red wine, and/or British red wine

1 part fresh fairtrade lemon juice

1 part fresh fairtrade orange juice

1 part organic orange-based liqueur
2 parts fairtrade caster sugar
Sliced fairtrade citrus fruits to taste
Sliced organic, locally-grown apples to taste
Fizzy natural British spring water

Combine all ingredients except the water and stir well so that the sugar dissolves properly, then leave in a cool place, covered with a cloth or solid object for a short time before your reception. When the time comes to serve the drinks place some ice in with mixture and add as much of the fizzy water as you like. Serve with a ladle into guests' glasses.

Non-alcoholic drinks

Really, the sky is the limit with non-alcoholic drinks. I've looked at dozens and dozens of recipes for non-alcoholic cocktails and there are so many variants I could fill up this whole book just with them.

Your best bet is to experiment with various flavours, mixing them as you go. Even if we just stick to British-grown, organic juices and cordials along with British grown, organic accompaniments, there are endless combinations of flavours that work particularly well together. Add some fresh, fairtrade citrus and soft fruit juices and cordials and you have a multitude of choices to satisfy all tastes.

If you are doing the drinks yourself and have a large juicer — or your caterers do — you can make some stunning combinations which can be diluted with organic fizzy lemonade or ginger ale to create delicious party drinks — without the booze. And even when it comes to the toast and speeches, if you don't want alcoholic drinks you can create just as festive a feel with organic fizzy apple or white grape juice.

Let's consider some of the more obvious and popular combinations:

- Apple and blackberry
- Apple and lemon
- Apple and carrot
- Apple and pineapple
- Apple and peach
- Apple and apricot
- Carrot and sweet red pepper (one of my favourites!)
- Carrot, red pepper and strawberry
- Carrot and orange
- Orange and tomato
- Orange and grapefruit
- Mango and pineapple
- Mango and lemon
- Mango and orange
- Mango and lime
- White grape and apple
- White grape and mango
- White grape and apricot
- White grape and strawberry
- White grape and raspberry
- White grape and blackberry

- Red grape and carrot

- Red grape and apple

- Red grape and apricot

- ... and so it goes on.

Don't forget to ensure that you serve fairtrade and/or organic **tea and coffee**, too. And in the summer you might want to serve iced tea as a non-alcoholic beverage — it's delicious either plain, or with one of dozens of possible flavourings.

Iced tea really couldn't be easier to make; there are numerous recipes available on the internet (key "iced tea recipes" into your favourite search engine) but essentially all you need to do is brew tea in the ordinary way — somewhat on the strong side — and cool it.

After that you will combine it with ice and flavourings such as honey to sweeten, and any number of fruit and herb additions that make it extra special. The most popular of these are fresh, organic/fairtrade peach juice or purée, mint, organic British apple juice, fairtrade citrus juices, and organic British summer soft fruits.

Drinks

What you can do

- Decide how you feel about the balance amongst organic, fairtrade, sustainable, biodynamic and British-produced drinks, and make your decisions accordingly.

- Accept that there are drinks in almost all categories that are labelled "organic", but not all will be as green as you might like them to be.

- Realise that "sustainable" drink products are helpful but can involve many thousands of "food miles".

- Know that "biodynamic" wines are a great idea but the methods involved need to stabilise before they can become more widely available.

- Know that although beer or cider may not be organic, it can be produced on a very local basis to that of where you're holding your reception.

- Be aware that organic spirits and liqueurs exist in the UK, as well as a good choice of organic fortified wines.

- Be aware that despite not all British wine production being organic, it does a lot to promote local business which is an important step in eco-consumerism.

- If you do not want alcohol at your wedding reception, be aware that the choice of organic, locally-sourced non-alcoholic drinks in the UK is vast — and delicious.

- Think twice about going for screw-topped wine bottles; old-fashioned corks are not as eco-unfriendly as some businesses might make them out to be.

- Don't be afraid to experiment with cocktails, as long as they're made from organic or at least fairtrade/eco-friendly ingredients.

- With non-alcoholic drinks, benefit from organic, fairtrade and/or locally produced options.

- Don't forget to include organic and/or fairtrade tea and coffee on your menu.

12 Photography

When contemplating this chapter I wondered just how much there would be to say on the "green" elements of photography, other than the obvious point of traditional film and film development involving potentially nasty chemicals. With that sort of traditional photography now largely replaced by the much cleaner digital variety, it was beginning to look like a very short chapter indeed.

I was surprised, therefore, to find out that some wedding photographers regard the whole green issue on a much broader basis, and there is very much more to eco-friendly photography than meets the eye.

I interviewed Berkshire-based **Andrew Sansom** — one of the most respected and highly regarded wedding photographers in the south-east of the UK — to find out more, and here is how our conversation went:

Andrew, what exactly is not "green" about traditional photography? Chemicals used in processing? Manufacturing of film stock?

The key non-green feature of traditional photography is the reliance on chemicals during every stage of the process.

The image capturing layers of **the film itself** contain minute grains of silver-halide crystals that act as the photon detectors. Silver-halide grains are manufactured by combining silver-nitrate and halide salts (chloride, bromide and iodide). These grains are then chemically modified to increase their light sensitivity. The grains are bound together, and to the plastic part of the film with gelatine, so are not vegetarian friendly either.

The development step which turns the film into slides or negatives uses yet more chemicals.

The developing is stopped either by washing or with a stop bath. The unexposed silver-halide grains are removed using a fixing solution. The silver that was developed in the first step is removed by bleaching chemicals. The negative image is then washed to remove as much of the chemicals and reaction products as possible. The film strips are then dried.

The printing step involves oxidised developer molecules combining with the colour-forming couplers to create a silver image and a dye image. The reaction is stopped by a washing step.

The silver image and any remaining unexposed silver halide are removed in a combined bleach-plus-fix solution. The resulting print is then washed to remove any residual chemicals.

The various chemicals are all environmentally hazardous. Once they have been used to process film, the chemicals must be immediately discarded in an environmentally sound way according to the environmental protection law of the country. Because it is expensive to do so, film processing companies can be tempted to just pour the chemicals down the drain.

Another environmental "weakness" of traditional photography is the need to refrigerate unused film to maintain its quality and ensure necessary longevity of life.

Okay, it's easy to see why digital photography is "greener", but are there are eco-downsides to it?

Digital photography is "greener" in terms of using far less chemicals, but the other environmental downsides can be just as bad.

Even small cameras can use a considerable amount of electricity, either through normal or rechargeable batteries. Once you add in the electricity usage of your computer, other electronic storage devices, monitor, printer, and various chargers etc., you can end up consuming hundreds or thousands of kilowatt-hours of electricity a year.

Any office environment uses a large amount of paper — whatever happened to the paperless office we dreamt about 20 years ago? A business like photography can potentially use even more, as it is very easy to end up printing unnecessarily. Whether printing photos or documents, most printers have been designed so that the manufacturers make profits from selling plastic cartridges with miniscule amounts of ink, and we are expected to continually buy new cartridges.

The other significant non-green aspect of modern photography is the replacing of electronic equipment. We have become accustomed to the idea of equipment being obsolete within a couple years and sometimes less. Often this discarded equipment contains harmful metals and chemicals which affect the environment if not correctly disposed of or recycled. Even the obtaining of these metals and chemicals can have an environmental impact, e.g. a key metal in mobile phones is mined in areas of Africa where critically endangered gorillas live.

So what steps are you taking to make your professional wedding photography as "green" as possible?

I run my car (for business and private use) on bio-diesel. This is important as a typical wedding can involve 300 miles of driving by the time I have visited to show my work, visited again to discuss the details before the wedding, attended the rehearsal and visited all venues, attended on the day, and visited to present the photos to the couple and family/friends.

All new purchases of paper, office stationery and printer inks are from recycled sources. I also reuse or recycle wherever possible packaging that has been sent to me.

All batteries used are now rechargeable. This has been a significant change as it is possible to use eight AA batteries in the camera flash during a wedding.

I have recently begun sending excessive packaging (in size or use of plastic) back to manufacturers to encourage improvements, as well as actively campaigning on issues such as climate change, recycling, and avoiding palm oil (killing orang-utans).

I am on the steering committee for an annual Borough Council-led Environmental Clean-up around local rivers and canals, a member of the local Business-Community partnership that links business and charities, and donate framed photographs to various charitable fundraisers.

Long-lived equipment is environmentally friendly. Now that digital technology is just as good as traditional, I will not be replacing any equipment until I genuinely need to due to it wearing out or no longer being adequate. Any equipment replaced will be donated so it can be reused elsewhere.

The basic energy tips you're practising in your non-photo life will work in the studio, too. Using compact fluorescent bulbs and taking a degree or two off the thermostat in winter (and adding a degree in summer) will save energy and keep hundreds of pounds of CO_2 out of the atmosphere.

Where appropriate I'm providing images to brides and grooms on memory stick rather than CDs. As well as being more efficient for me, the memory stick is more likely to be reused than CDs or a DVD.

All images are provided electronically with no need for printing, and put online for family and friends to view. A traditional album is an optional extra, and photobooks are now being offered which use fewer resources.

I have given my time to charity work in the UK and Africa, including reforestation and water projects in Kenya.

Also, I am investigating the possibility of offering my clients a green alternative to traditional wedding albums, such as a wedding album made from all recycled materials. There are several online that I intend investigating.

At the same time I am looking at greener framing and mounting options.

I intend donating directly to the reforestation project in Kenya as a means of offsetting my business and private CO_2 emissions. We cannot separate our business and private actions and have to be as green as we can in all areas of our lives.

I use local resources and businesses whenever it is possible. The office I share uses 100% renewable electricity and I intend moving my home to a renewable supplier very soon.

Now — what advice would you give to amateur wedding photographers to help them stay as "green" as they can?

One key point I must make is that anyone using an amateur photographer for their wedding is taking a significant risk on the quality of the photos they will receive!

Any photographer whether professional or amateur should have the following:

- spare camera;
- spare batteries for cameras and for flash;

- spare memory cards, and enough cards for several hundred photos;

- a clear understanding of the style of photos the couple want, and how obtrusive they are prepared for the photographer to be;

- professional indemnity and public liability insurance;

- be familiar with all venues to get the best photos irrespective of weather conditions;

- make themselves familiar with any special family situations, and key people to be included in photos, e.g. surviving grandparents, god-parents etc.

Here are some other photography tips:

- Use the viewer on the back of the camera as little as possible, as it is the greediest consumer of energy in the camera. You may also miss excellent photos while reviewing ones you've already taken.

- Use flash sparingly to conserve batteries, and provide minimal dis-traction particularly during the service.

- Adjust the camera to take account of different lighting, i.e. white balance. A white wedding dress can look different – colours depending on whether it is outdoors, under fluorescent lights, under normal lights etc.

- Make back-up copies of all photos as soon as practical after taking them, and keep the copies away from the originals. If anything hap-pens to the memory cards without a backup having been taken, there might not be any photos to show the couple.

Any further advice for brides and grooms?

Avoid the trend to put disposable cameras on tables. In addition to using film, it is obvious how environmentally unfriendly their construction and single use is. Instead, ask friends to share their digital photos with all the guests through an online facility like **Flickr** or even on **Facebook**.

Buying everything from locally owned businesses can be extended to wedding photography as well. You'll be supporting a local business and limiting the carbon footprint of your wedding.

Andrew can be contacted at: http://www.andrewsansom.com/Weddings.htm.

Interesting food for thought

There are couple of points I would like to add to Andrew's information, as follows. One, although of course it is very wasteful to provide single-use disposable cameras for guests to use, as I understand it, at the time of writing, it is now possible to recycle these devices, via Kodak. The second point is that in addition to uploading your wedding photos to Flickr or Facebook, you can also make good use of your wedding website (see Chapter 4).

Wedding videos

There is not much to add to this element of your wedding that Andrew hasn't covered in his very comprehensive advice about stills photography, as the two disciplines do share a good few common elements, e.g.

in the use of electricity, batteries, renewal of equipment, use of memory sticks rather than CDs and DVDs, etc.

As for enabling all and sundry to view the wedding video, as Flickr and Facebook are to still photos, YouTube and your own wedding website are to the motion picture version! If you are using a wedding website facility it's worth checking that the website they build for you is capable of supporting video. If you are building a site yourself you may not be able to include video, depending on the nature of the site, but I believe you can link to YouTube from there.

Another point worth considering when contemplating your wedding video is that the old adage of "film is cheap so shoot plenty — you can always edit it afterwards" is no longer appropriate, at least in eco-friendly terms. Although obviously nowadays no-one would actually shoot on film, there is still the issue of electrical energy being used to generate the basic digital material, and being used to edit it afterwards. As for copies of your wedding video, try as far as you can to suggest guests and other interested parties download it from your wedding website or YouTube — sending out DVDs or even memory sticks is more wasteful.

If you're using professional videographers you might like to ask them to keep their raw shooting down to a reasonable level and to work to a carefully planned shot list so that there is a minimum of wastage, and the least possible amount of editing is required later. Ironically, amateur videographers tend to shoot in much shorter bursts which although creatively perhaps not so appealing, in energy terms is less wasteful.

Photography

What you can do

- At all costs avoid using any traditional photography methods involving film and processing chemicals.

- Ensure that all batteries used in camera equipment are rechargeable.

- Try to ensure that flash is used as little as possible.

- Avoid using the viewer on a digital camera as much as possible, as it uses a lot of energy.

- Do not provide disposable cameras for guests to use and discourage anyone wanting to bring their own.

- Upload your photos to your wedding website or platforms such as Flickr or Facebook.

- Ask guests and other interested parties to view the photos on there, rather than have prints done.

- Use memory sticks, not CDs or DVDs, to transfer both still and video images where required.

- When photo prints are required, keep these to a minimum.

- Encourage people to download your video to their computers, not receive it on DVD or even memory stick.

13 Transportation

By transportation here, I mean the transportation you use to get your-selves and your guests to and from your wedding ceremony, the reception, and all other relevant points.

Although the greener options for transporting yourselves and your guests to and from your wedding may seem obvious enough — avoid cars, use public transport where possible — **it isn't actually that simple** — or that obvious.

For example, taking a diesel train (many of the smaller routes are covered by these) is probably more polluting in the case of an average family than it would be for them to make the same trip in a so-called "gas-guzzling" SUV/4x4.

There are even scientists and politicians busily calculating the emissions caused in producing the food you'd need for the energy to walk a given distance — in terms of your calorie consumption linked to dairy herds, meat farming, etc — and saying that in some circumstances this would be up to four times more polluting overall, than it would be for you to drive the same distance in a small car.

As for everyone pointing the accusing emissions finger at the airlines, it is a generally undisputed fact that cows produce more in the way of harmful gases than the airlines do.

So how do you work out the greenest methods of transport realistically?

Transport for your guests

Once again, you need to balance the more obvious green ways of travelling with practical considerations and common sense, and although obviously you can't dictate how your guests are going to travel, you can at least encourage them to choose greener options.

People **flying in from abroad** should be encouraged to combine your wedding with a holiday in the region, so getting the most out of their air travel. You can also suggest carbon offset ideas to them and if necessary, say you would rather they paid for carbon offset than bring you a wedding gift. (See Chapter 14.)

If you have largish groups coming from the same place, you could organise one or more **coaches** to pick them up from a central point, take them to and from the wedding and return them later. It's likely that the cost per head of doing that should not be more than the cost of driving, and there are added advantages to guests — e.g. no parking problems, door-to-door transport, no worries about drink-driving, etc.

Unless you are very well off financially, guests should not expect you to pay for this service, especially as were they to make their own way to your wedding they would have to pick up the cost themselves. You could, however, provide a little entertainment for them on the way there and back; for example, a sing-song or karaoke competition to get them in the mood for a great party!

If there is a convenient **railway station** near the wedding venue you can suggest appropriate trains for guests to get from various points and organise a minibus to pick them up and return them. Once again there are other advantages to guests apart from keeping pollution down.

As we've covered earlier in the book, the ideal arrangement from the eco-friendly point of view is for wedding ceremony and reception to be within walking distance of one another, and even better, in the same place. If there is a walk involved, it makes sense to gather together as many **umbrellas** as possible and have them on hand for ushers/groomsmen to hand out to guests if it's raining. If rain is forecast guests *should* take their own precautions, but people being people, the majority won't!

Transporting yourselves and the wedding party

If the distance from where you are staying to the wedding ceremony and reception is only short, frankly, the pollution caused by a reasonable car taking you there isn't going to make the world grind to a halt. Okay, you probably won't want to hire one of these huge stretch Hummers or other limousines, although even they wouldn't burn up that much in emission terms over a journey of a few miles. But they do tend to scream "wasteful" at the top of their lurid voices.

If you prefer, you can choose to hire one or more **eco-friendly cars** – ones which run on LPG, bio-diesel, etc. – and at the time of writing there are numerous car hire companies in the UK offering such a service, both self-drive and chauffeur-driven. Key "car hire"+"eco-friendly" into your favourite search engine.

Another option is to use **electric cars**. Obviously like any other form of motorised transport these do involve the consumption of some sort of energy, but at least pollution is kept to a minimum. Currently it is possible to hire electric cars, also both self-drive and chauffeur-driven. Key "electric car hire" into your favourite search engine.

However, you may choose to make a more distinctive statement in your choice of transport, and here's where there are a few alternatives – some perhaps more practical than others.

First of all, you could choose a fleet of **bicycle rickshaws**. Popular for many years in various eastern countries, these are now appearing more and more in the UK as non-polluting transportation. For availability in your area, key "bicycle rickshaws" into your favourite search engine.

Some bridal couples fancy the romantic notion of leaving the ceremony and/or reception together on either a **motorcycle or a tandem bicycle**. Although I can see the point of doing this both in romantic and eco-friendly terms, the practicalities of getting a bride in full wedding gown on to either device are probably not worth the headaches. If you do decide on either of these options, be sure to choose clothing that is unlikely to be damaged or torn.

Now, the next issue is **horse-drawn vehicles**. I have to put my hands up here and admit that in my last weddings book, *The A to Z of Wedding Worries and how to put them right*, I was less than enthusiastic about this option, largely for safety reasons. So no-one can call me a hypocrite, I reproduce here exactly what I said there!

Animals: horse-drawn transport, is it safe?

I know lots of people these days fancy the idea of being driven to the ceremony and to the reception in a beautiful horse-drawn carriage, or even in a small cart pulled by a pony. I know there are numerous companies that specialise in supplying horse-drawn vehicles for weddings and make a good living out of it.

I also know horses and ponies very well, having ridden them most of my life and known many people who are into carriage driving.

If this is something you are contemplating, I hate to be a killjoy, but think carefully. Unless it's an experienced wedding carriage puller, even the most placid and laid-back horse or pony is unlikely to be comfortable with crowds of people waving and shouting excitedly. And even those experienced carriage pullers can be spooked by a car backfiring or other sudden, loud noise.

You might think that a couple of dear old cart horses couldn't possibly be anything other than sweetness and light as they pull you to your dream wedding. But if you have ever seen a couple of 19 hand Shires spook at full gallop (I have, and it's terrifying) you may prefer to consider a more mechanical option.

If after all my wet-blanket ravings you still want to go the horse-drawn route, here's my advice.

Horse-drawn wedding vehicle companies

There are many of these around and you'll find them in your local Yellow Pages or online via Google or other search engine.

Having got to know the people and horses involved in quite a successful such company local to me, I have to say, check carefully and get some personal recommendations first. The company I got to know used young, inexperienced horses and equally young (therefore cheap) and inexperienced drivers. In the main they got away with it when they had wedding groups on board but they did have some dreadful accidents when loading and unloading horses and vehicles.

Ask the company for references and also visit their yard and ask to meet their horses. If the horses look calm, clean and in good health you're probably OK. Beware horses that seem shy, skittish, sweated up, underweight, or with scars on their heads and other harness areas of their bodies (mainly the neck, shoulders and back).

Private horse-drawn vehicles

Ironically this may be the better option, especially if you know the horse's owner well and trust him or her and his/her judgment. A privately owned horse is likely to be more of a docile pet than one owned by a carriage yard and is also likely to have a better relationship with its owner/driver.

Almost certainly the owner will want to rehearse the journey with the horse (beware if s/he doesn't) so it doesn't encounter any surprises on the day. You might enjoy going along for the ride, if you have time, to make sure you don't have any previously unknown qualms about horse-drawn transport. Also, assuming the vehicle used for the rehearsal is the same one to be used on the day, you can check out realistically how easy or hard it will be to climb up into and down from the vehicle in your wedding attire.

On the day, it's a good idea to warn as many of your bridal party and guests as possible that you will be arriving and departing via real, live horsepower, and tell them not to do anything that could cause a fright.

There you go – *mea culpa*. But whatever my safety concerns might be, it can't be argued that horse-drawn transport is greener than the motorised variety, although of course horses produce unpleasant gases rather in the way that cows do. As there are far fewer horses on the planet than there are cows, though, horses in all seriousness do not contribute hugely to global warming.

And for a country wedding on a lovely summer's day, the thought of the bride, groom and bridal party being conveyed to and from the proceedings in a fleet of horse-drawn vehicles — or one large omnibus type of cart pulled by a big, strong, sensible draught horse — is a lovely, romantic one. Bear in mind that horse-drawn vehicles usually are not as easy to get into and out of, so avoid any tight skirts or fancy footwear that could impede progress.

The next transportation-based issue we need to look at is connected with the honeymoon, but as that involves other things besides transport, I've given that a chapter of its own — see Chapter 14.

Transportation

What you can do

- Be aware that public transport isn't always greener than going by car.
- Encourage guests travelling by air to maximise their stay and pay for carbon offset.
- Organise a coach to take larger groups of guests to your wedding.
- Encourage guests to arrive by train — have them picked up by minibus.
- For the bridal party, hire eco-friendly/electric cars.
- Consider using bicycle rickshaws.
- Consider using a motorbike or tandem bicycle for bride and groom.
- Consider horse-drawn transport, but be safety conscious.

14 Honeymoon

When it comes to green issues, of all topics that tend to hit the headlines **travel** is probably the most frequently seen in the newspaper headlines. Wherever we go — even if we walk there and back — a certain amount of energy is used and nearly always, a certain amount of undesirable gases or fumes is released into the atmosphere.

Realistically, though, we are not going to stop travelling altogether. Now that most of us have experienced trips abroad and holidays in somewhat friendlier climates than those we experience in the UK, only some of us are prepared to forego the opportunity to see other (warmer) parts of the world — especially when we're honeymooning, which really should be the holiday to end all holidays.

Of course, many of us do enjoy the **British climate and beautiful scenery**, and are more than delighted to steal away for a romantic honeymoon in a picturesque country cottage or glorious National Trust venue not far away from where we live. The sportier types are happy to honeymoon under canvass in one or more of Britain's many beauty spots, or travel a relatively short distance by public transport to a British location to take part in things like rock climbing, hiking, pony trekking or any one of numerous other outdoor activities — several of which I have already pointed out in Chapter 2, in connection with hen and stag celebrations.

However, the temptation to go beyond the shores of the British Isles for your honeymoon can still be strong, and despite the need for travel, there are still ways of making such honeymoons as green as possible.

Travel within Europe

Honeymooning on continental Europe **by car** is pretty easy nowadays, but unless you're driving an eco-friendly car it does seem to be a little on the wasteful side. And bear in mind, too, that the eco-fuels your eco-friendly car might use are not necessarily going to be readily available wherever you travel in Europe — well, certainly not at the time of writing, anyway.

A preferable consideration is **public transport**. Although our trains in the UK currently can leave a bit to be desired, train services in continental Europe tend to be far better and more efficient. At the same time, too, travel by train can be pretty economical in comparison with travelling the same routes by private car. If you're camping, say, or backpacking/hostelling/B&B-ing, such a honeymoon can enable you to see many of the stunning sights of European cities and countryside at relatively low cost ... not only to the environment, but also to your wallets.

Even if you say to hell with cheaper options and decide to spoil yourselves, train transport to some of Europe's most romantic cities is still a financially and ecologically viable option and depending on season and circumstances, relatively luxurious hotel accommodation can be obtained for reasonable rates ... without compromising on sumptuous surroundings and an utterly magical stay.

Beyond Europe

If you want to honeymoon — or, indeed, get married and then combine that trip with a honeymoon — beyond Europe, don't despair. Although the ultra-green finger-waggers may target you for such activities, these do not necessarily have to be deleterious to the planet.

Before we go any further, I suppose we ought to look at **air travel** and take its consequences into consideration.

Okay, air travel has received huge amounts of bad press recently. If you really want to know how air travel impacts on the planet in terms of CO_2 emissions, you need to look at the following website which at the time of writing gives you some stark statistics on the problem:

http://climatecare.org/calculators/flight

And going by sea is not by any means the answer, either.

Although a gentle cruise in a narrow boat along a picturesque British canal or a small craft cruising around on the Norfolk Broads for a few days won't cause too much in the way of CO_2 emission problems, large **cruise and/or passenger ships** are anything but green.

Per passenger mile, it seems very large cruise or passenger ships emit nearly twice the amount of CO_2 than there would be caused by an average long-haul flight, and that's taking into consideration the further damage aircraft pollution does to the higher parts of our atmosphere. A sobering thought. And this is a conservative estimate, as some people say the figure is much higher — one source I read claimed that going to north-eastern USA from the UK in a very large passenger ship creates over seven times the carbon emissions that there would be if you made the same journey by plane.

Passenger ships are somewhat unfriendly in other eco-areas, too, polluting the waters through which they travel, although many cruise and passenger ship lines have cleaned up their acts quite noticeably since the USA began imposing huge fines on them for being eco-dirty in their territorial waters. At the time of writing, however, regulations about pollution from ships are nowhere nearly as stringent elsewhere in the world.

Another issue with cruise ships is that apart from providing some tourists to buy souvenirs, ice creams and maybe the odd meal or drink, they do not tend to contribute much to the communities they visit other than by leaving their rubbish behind. And the rubbish they generate is phenomenal: an average seven day cruise can generate several dozen tonnes of actual rubbish, nearly 40,000 gallons of oil-filthy water, more than 200,000 gallons of sewage, and over a million tonnes of waste water.

Carbon offset

What has become very popular in recent times is the whole issue of **carbon offset**, whereby if you pay to plant a tree or contribute towards another green cause you can counter-balance your CO_2 emissions caused by travel.

Needless to say numerous commercial enterprises have seen the potential for big business here, playing on the guilt of regular long distance travellers and offering all sorts of carbon offset schemes. Without wishing to besmirch genuine businesses in this field, the reality is that some are less effective — and less trustworthy — than others.

Michael Bloch is the author of **GreenLivingTips.com**, an eco-lifestyle resource powered by renewable energy and offering a wide variety of earth friendly tips, green guides, advice and environment related news. He has written an extremely useful article about buying carbon offsets and kindly has allowed me to reproduce it here. His advice is excellent.

Buying carbon offsets

By Michael Bloch

GreenLivingTips.com

The carbon offsetting industry is suffering somewhat of tarnished image at the moment due to some unscrupulous operators and organizations who start out with the right intentions, but can't deliver. Many well-meaning people are wasting their hard earned cash in the belief that their purchase is offsetting their carbon dioxide emission footprint.

The problem with the carbon offset industry is that governments have been slow to react in regulating it and what measures have been in place for certification have often been inadequate. This particularly applies where trees are involved in carbon offset programs.

Offsetting your carbon emissions remains an important gesture and sponsoring the planting of trees is a wonderful way to do so, so here's some tips to help ensure the money you spend actually has some benefit to the environment.

The first thing to bear in mind about buying trees as carbon offsets are that they should be considered as a last resort option; i.e. try everything you can to reduce your carbon emissions first, such as the use of CFL bulbs or even LED's for lighting; efficient use of hot water systems; addressing phantom power loads and reducing meat consumption – there's so much you can do that can actually save you money while benefiting the environment.

Many of the tips on GreenLivingTips.com are related to reducing carbon emission reduction. Generally speaking, it boils down to this – consumption = carbon dioxide. The less processing of an item, the less transport, the less carbon emissions are generated.

Having reduced your carbon footprint as much as possible, now it's time to offset what you can't.

I'm all for planting trees, any excuse is good – we've wiped out so many forests in our greed that it's going to take a long time to restore the damage we've done. Where I live, South Australia, we managed to clear around 133,000 square kilometres of bushland for agricultural and other purposes in under 100 years. Much of what wasn't cleared in this state was desert anyway and some of what has been cleared may as well be desert as it's been damaged so badly. One of the best known and once most prolific types of trees in South Australia is the Mallee which take decades to mature.

Carbon offset purchase tips

The following are tips, things to look for and questions to ask a prospective provider to help ensure the environment is benefiting and you are getting your money's worth – not simply lining some entrepreneur's pockets to help them buy a carbon spewing Ferrari:

- Do some research on the company you're considering buying from via your favourite search engine. Try entering: companyname.scam

When you review the results, take the opinions you read with a grain of salt. Is any "dirt" you find specifically about that company or just about carbon offsetting generally? There are plenty of naysayers around.

- A good offset company will also provide carbon emission reduction tips on their site. It indicates a level of passion about the issue rather than just a moneymaking exercise. Beware of any company that is heavy on the "feelgood" and light on the reality and facts of tree planting.

- What types of trees will be planted? They should be species that won't damage the local ecosystem. Some plantations that use non-native trees create more environmental problems than they address.

- Some offset companies are registered charities, that makes any offsets you purchase a personal tax deduction in most countries; but you'll need to buy them from a local provider. In most countries, it doesn't matter where you buy your offsets from in connection with your business as it becomes an operating expense and will be tax deductible anyway.

- Are the trees you're "buying" actually being propagated from seed, or are they existing trees that were slated for conservation anyway?

- How does the offsetting company or organization record the trees; is there the possibility the same tree is being sold twice? This does happen.

- Is the company definitive in where the trees will be planted? Can they provide any evidence of the planting?

- How long after you've paid your money until the trees will be planted? I've read of some companies obtaining cash for tree planting projects that won't commence for years.

- What's the survival rate of the trees they plant? Nobody can guarantee a seedling will survive through to maturity, so how do they address that issue?

- Will the trees be cut down in the future and what sorts of guarantees are in place that they won't be before they've at least absorbed the CO_2 they were meant to? If they are to be utilized, for what purpose? The carbon must continue to be stored in the wood (e.g. building) or wind up in the soil to have made the sequestration of benefit.

- Does the program have any sort of government backing or certification/endorsement from a respected industry association?

- Certificates and bumper stickers are all very nice bonuses in these schemes; but keep your focus on the organization's tree planting practices; after all, you're wanting to spend your cash on offsetting your carbon footprint, not on postage, printing and paper... and just on that issue; if they do provide a certificate, is it on recycled paper?

- Think global when selecting a provider; that's why it's called global warming, not local warming. While paying for trees to be planted in your own country is great, there's some excellent tree planting programs in developing countries where given decreased labour costs and favourable exchange rates, you can have more trees planted for your money. Perhaps you can sponsor local projects in one transaction and an overseas project in another. An additional bonus is that you'll also be likely helping an impoverished community. A word of warning though, these tree planting programs in developing countries do tend to be a little riskier, so should be scrutinized carefully. Also check that local indigenous communities have not been forcibly displaced for the planting project.

You really shouldn't need to have to ask the provider all the above questions; most of them should be addressed on their site. The more questions you need to ask, the less likely that it's all above board.

Do bear in mind that a tree's ability to absorb carbon dioxide will greatly vary on location, the type of tree and it may take many, many years before that tree would have absorbed the level of carbon dioxide you've generated in a single year. For that reason, it's important to ensure you deal with reputable organizations who have a real commitment to the industry for the long term, not just those who stick seedlings in the ground and forget about them.

The carbon offset industry is relatively new and as such, it's somewhat of a Wild West scenario where anything goes. Regardless of what the naysayers may spout, buying trees through an ethical offset provider is a valid and beneficial contribution to the environment. Just spend a little time in research and asking questions before you settle on who you spend your cash with. After all, it's not just about alleviating guilt; it's about helping restore the damage we've collectively done to this planet.

Trees are wonderful, but remember: consumption = carbon dioxide; and reducing consumption of non-essential items is the best step any of us can take in addressing global warming.

On his website, Michael has published dozens of other helpful articles about all aspects of green living, so do give it a surf — http://www.GreenLivingTips.com.

Eco tourism

So, now that I have all but crucified any form of long distance travel other than on foot or perhaps by camel, what if you still feel it's important to go abroad?

Apart from using a respectable carbon offset facility, you can choose a destination that meets the main criteria of eco tourism. To define this, let me quote from the website of The International Ecotourism Society (TIES) (http://www.ecotourism.org) who say: "uniting communities, conservation and sustainable travel, TIES promotes responsible travel to natural areas that conserves the environment and improves the well-being of local people."

Of course even a definition as well-structured as this is still open to some fairly creative interpretation and unless I am being overly cynical, it's likely that there are businesses in this area trying to climb on to the green bandwagon without necessarily fulfilling as many green criteria as we would like.

In one press story I read recently it was stated that to qualify for membership of a "green tourism" initiative launched in a popular area of southern England, all hotels had to do was prove they recycled some of their waste and used energy-efficient light bulbs.

However, proper eco-tourism initiatives do exist and are expanding in number and nature every day, all over the world — from Africa to South America to the Himalayas to the Poles. To find out the latest opinions from specialist journalists on which current options really are of value, key "eco tourism" into your favourite search engine and look for recent press articles on the subject. To get a picture of what is available commercially, key in either "eco resorts", "eco tours" or "eco honeymoons".

Honeymoon

What you can do

- Obviously the closer to home, in the main, the greener the honeymoon from a travel point of view, at least.

- Consider a romantic getaway in the UK.

- Where possible travel by public transport in the UK and within Europe (trains, coaches).

- Be aware that air travel is very eco-dirty.

- Be aware that large cruise or passenger ships are even eco-dirtier.

- If you are travelling by air or ship, buy some carbon offsets.

- Choose your carbon offset company very carefully.

- If you want to go a long distance away, consider an eco tourism option.

- If choosing eco tourism, check out current views on what is and is not genuine in the quality press online.

15: Resources

This isn't really a chapter as such — more a list of resources and further reading that you might find helpful. In each chapter of the book you'll see that where relevant I give you the words you need to key into your favourite search engine to bring up the most recent searches when you read this book. Don't forget to include the quotation marks/inverted commas when I have indicated they should be used, as I pointed out in the Introduction.

Please note that websites listed are current at the time of writing, but may not be current by the time you read this book. So without further ado ...

Websites

Confetti

http://www.confettidirect.co.uk

Drinks

http://www.britishcassis.co.uk
http://www.winesofinterest.co.uk/organics.htm
http://www.vineorganic.co.uk
http://www.vintageroots.co.uk/biodynamic.asp
http://www.english-wine.com
http://www.defra.gov.uk/foodrin/wine/industry.htm
http://www.ukwinesites.com
http://www.aboutorganics.co.uk
http://www.buyorganics.co.uk
http://www.alotoforganics.co.uk
http://www.sustainweb.org
http://www.organic-champagne.co.uk
http://www.localflavour.co.uk
http://www.organics-on-line.com
http://www.clipper-teas.com

Fashion

http://www.enamore.co.uk
http://www.oxfam.org.uk
http://www.sellmyweddingdress.co.uk
http://www.friendly-wedding-directory.co.uk

http://www.ethical-junction.org
http://www.hettyrose.co.uk
http://www.viridisluxe.com
http://peopletree.co.uk
http://www.greenfibres.com
http://www.greenfibres.org
http://www.peopletree.co.uk
http://www.adili.com
http://www.greenknickers.org
http://www.ebay.co.uk

Food, organic/local

http://www.farmshop.uk.com
http://www.littlelocalfood.com
http://www.localfoodworks.org
http://www.thelfd.com
http://www.slowfood.org.uk
http://www.foodfullstop.com
http://www.bigbarn.co.uk
http://www.farmersmarkets.net
http://www.lfm.org.uk
http://www.scottishfarmersmarkets.co.uk
http://www.scottishfoodanddrink.com
http://www.fmiw.co.uk
http://www.whyorganic.org
http://www.farma.org.uk
http://www.soilassociation.org
http://www.soilassociationscotland.org
http://www.organic.aber.ac.uk
http://www.organicassistant.com
http://www.locavores.com

http://www.cooperatives-uk.coop
http://www.bigbarn.co.uk
http://www.greencuisine.penrhos.com
http://www.vegsoc.org/cordonvert/recipes

Gemstone and precious metal mining, jewellery

http://www.globalwitness.org
http://www.greenkarat.com

General

http://www.eco-friendlyweddings.co.uk
http://www.greenunion.co.uk
http://www.ethicalweddings.com
http://www.carbon-info.org
http://www.greatgreenwedding.com
http://www.britishinformation.com/eco-friendly-weddings
http://www.allthingseco.co.uk
http://www.ecostreet.com
http://www.greenlivingtips.com
http://www.foe.co.uk
http://www.cat.org.uk
http://www.ethicalsuperstore.com
http://www.naturalcollection.com
http://footprint.wwf.org.uk
http://www.freecycle.org
http://www.edibleflavours.co.uk
http://www.biobags.co.uk
http://www.scarredearth.co.uk
http://www.care2.com
http://www.ecomoon.co.uk

Gifts

http://www.giveit.co.uk
http://www.thealternativeweddinglist.co.uk
http://www.smartlygreen.com
http://www.ecokettle.com
http://www.allthingsgreen.net
http://www.ourgreenweddinglist.com
http://www.goodgifts.org

Invitations

http://www.evite.co.uk

Organic cosmetics

http://www.lovelula.com
http://www.bare-faced-cheek.co.uk
http://www.chemicalsafeskincare.co.uk

Photography

http://www.andrewsansom.com

Reception items

http://www.banthebulb.org
http://www.friendly-planet.co.uk
http://www.treecycle.com
http://www.cater4you.co.uk
http://www.kettlerscottagecrafts.co.uk

Transport /Travel

http://www.chooseclimate.org
http://www.climatecare.org
http://www.ichauffeur.co.uk/eco/climatecare
http://www.britishdrivingsociety.co.uk (horses!)
http://www.climatecare.org/calculators
http://www.ecotourism.org
http://www.guardian.co.uk/travel/green
http://www.green-business.co.uk/

Other books about eco-friendly weddings

Green Weddings that don't Cost the Earth by Carol Reed-Jones, Paper Crane Press, ISBN 0-9650833-0-6 (written and published in the USA)
Eco-Chic Weddings by Emily Elizabeth Anderson, Hatherleigh Press, ISBN 978-1-57826-240-3 (written and published in the USA)
Organic Weddings by Michelle Kozin, New Society Publishers, ISBN 0-86571-496-7 (written and published in the USA)

Useful green living books

The New Green Consumer Guide by Julia Hailes, Simon & Schuster UK Ltd., ISBN 978-0-7432-9530-7
The Rough Guide to Ethical Shopping by Duncan Clark, Rough Guides Ltd, ISBN 1-84353-265-4
Imperfectly Natural Woman by Janey Lee Grace, Crown House, ISBN 978-1904424895
Green Holiday Guides by ECEAT, Green Books http://www.greenbooks.co.uk

Organic Places to Stay in the UK by Linda Moss, Green Books, ISBN 978-1900322195

The Organic Directory by Clive Litchfield, Green Books, ISBN 978-1903998830

Other books about weddings from How To Books

Be the Best, Best Man & Make a Stunning Speech by Phillip Khan-Panni ISBN 978 1 85703 802 6

Get Wed for Less – A Bride's Guide by Liz Bright ISBN 978 1 84528 210 3

How To Go Carbon Neutral by Mark Brassington ISBN 978 1 84528 250 9

Making a Wedding Speech by John Bowden ISBN 978 1 84528 294 3

Making the Best Man's Speech by John Bowden ISBN 978 1 85703 659 6

Making the Bridegroom's Speech by John Bowden ISBN 978 1 85703 567 4

Making the Father of the Bride's Speech by John Bowden ISBN 978 1 85703 568 1

Planning A Wedding Reception at Home by Carol Godsmark ISBN 978 1 84528 295 0

The A to Z of Wedding Worries ... and how to put them right by Suzan St Maur ISBN 978 1 84528 172 4

The Complete Best Man by John Bowden ISBN 978 1 84528 104 5

Wedding Planner by Elizabeth Catherine Myers ISBN 978 1 84528 235 6

Wedding Speeches for Women by Suzan St Maur ISBN 978 1 84528 107 6

Index

Index